"Evangelical churches that are multisite or multiservice are like that for good-intentioned, pragmatic reasons. Jonathan Leeman challenges us to think exegetically and theologically about a popular practice that may not be as strategic as so many assume."

> **Andy Naselli,** Associate Professor of Systematic Theology and New Testament, Bethlehem College & Seminary

"Too often we don't think about what it means ̶ ̶ ̶ ̶a chu ̶ ̶ ̶ ̶ ̶ ̶ ̶ ̶rch together. Jonathan Leeman's book, th ̶ ̶ ̶ ̶fore, ̶ ̶ ̶ ̶ ̶ ̶ ̶ ̶ ̶ ̶ ̶ ̶ ̶ ̶ ̶ ̶ ̶ ̶d individualistic sensibilities. Still, L ̶ ̶ ̶ ̶ ̶ ̶ ̶ ̶ ̶ ̶ ̶ ̶ ̶e word *church* in the Scriptures means ̶ ̶ ̶ ̶ ̶ ̶ ̶ ̶ ̶ ̶ ̶ ̶assemble ̶e by definition two churches. The matt ̶ ̶ ̶ ̶ ̶ ̶ ̶ ̶ ̶ ̶people who love the Scriptures disagree, but I think Leeman ̶ ̶ ̶ ̶ ̶ ̶e is the most plausible."

> **Thomas R. Schreiner,** James Bucha ̶ ̶ ̶ ̶ ̶ ̶ ̶ ̶rison Professor of New Testament Interpretation, The Southern Baptist Theological Seminary

"*One Assembly* is more than a critique of the multiservice and multisite movement. Leeman persuasively argues for the biblical faithfulness, beauty, and effectiveness of a single church service. Instead of slowing down gospel growth, the single-service model actually promotes the Great Commission by encouraging church planting. This is a must-read for anyone interested in church growth."

> **Aaron Menikoff,** Senior Pastor, Mount Vernon Baptist Church, Sandy Springs, Georgia

"Jonathan Leeman clearly loves the church. He loves it enough to lay out here, with clarity and compassion, the one-assembly model that Scripture so consistently presents. Eminently engaging and stemming from deep personal experience, this book helpfully shows us not only what Scripture says a 'church' is but also how churches with multiple sites or services can move toward a single gathering. Leeman's carefully considered treatment is timely and relevant to all Christians, not just pastors and scholars."

> **Anne Rabe,** Former Lecturer in Classics, University of Kansas

"Leeman convincingly shows from Scripture and plain reason that a mark of the local church is *one assembly*, and churches do well to practice this biblical norm. I plead with church leaders to prayerfully hear Leeman's case so that Christ is more exalted, we are more faithful, and our churches most effectively advance the Great Commission."

> **P. J. Tibayan,** Pastor-Theologian, Bethany Baptist Church, Bellflower, California

"This book analyzes the multisite and multiservice model with tremendous commitment to Scripture, clarity, and precision. Jonathan Leeman brings to light the implications of the multisite and multiservice movement's chronological and geographical fragmentation of the one assembly: the redefinition of the nature of the church and the reshaping of the church morally. Every pastor must seriously consider his arguments."

Jonas Madureira, Senior Pastor, Word Baptist Church, São Paulo, Brazil

"Many churches take multiple services as a given. Increasingly, churches are embracing multisite models. With the boldness, courage, and zeal of a reformer, Jonathan Leeman invites us to submit our assumptions and practices in ministry to the scrutiny of what the Bible says about the church. Even if you don't agree with everything that *One Assembly* concludes about the church, Leeman is surely correct to call the church to build her life, worship, and service upon the foundation of Scripture alone. Let *One Assembly* provoke you, challenge you, and, above all, drive you to God's word."

Guy Prentiss Waters, James M. Baird Jr. Professor of New Testament, Reformed Theological Seminary, Jackson, Mississippi

"Jonathan Leeman has advanced significantly the discussion on what constitutes a local church. An *ekklēsia*, most fundamentally, is what it does: it is a gathering. Those looking to defend an alternative approach (either multisite or multiservice) will likely find some previously unconsidered arguments and data here. Leeman has assembled the most thorough case for one service/one church. Not everyone will be persuaded, of course; but Leeman's work was influential in our church's decision to move from multiservice to a single service."

Ryan Kelly, Pastor of Preaching, Desert Springs Church, Albuquerque, New Mexico

"The church of Jesus and the apostles cannot be redefined by our culture or our needs. This book describes the difficulties in my own experience of pastoring a multisite church that lost its building and was forced to split into six home campuses. Leeman provides an alternative for the multisite model, including the church-planting strategy our elders are preparing to follow. This book will challenge you and bless other church leaders in situations like mine."

Victor Shu, Lead Pastor, Radiant Grace Church, East Asia

ONE ASSEMBLY

Other 9Marks Books

The Rule of Love: How the Local Church Should Reflect God's Love and Authority, Jonathan Leeman (2018)

Church in Hard Places: How the Local Church Brings Life to the Poor and Needy, Mez McConnell and Mike McKinley (2016)

Why Trust the Bible?, Greg Gilbert (2015)

The Compelling Community: Where God's Power Makes a Church Attractive, Mark Dever and Jamie Dunlop (2015)

The Pastor and Counseling: The Basics of Shepherding Members in Need, Jeremy Pierre and Deepak Reju (2015)

Who Is Jesus?, Greg Gilbert (2015)

Nine Marks of a Healthy Church, 3rd edition, Mark Dever (2013)

Finding Faithful Elders and Deacons, Thabiti M. Anyabwile (2012)

Am I Really a Christian?, Mike McKinley (2011)

What Is the Gospel?, Greg Gilbert (2010)

Biblical Theology in the Life of the Church: A Guide for Ministry, Michael Lawrence (2010)

Church Planting Is for Wimps: How God Uses Messed-up People to Plant Ordinary Churches That Do Extraordinary Things, Mike McKinley (2010)

It Is Well: Expositions on Substitutionary Atonement, Mark Dever and Michael Lawrence (2010)

What Does God Want of Us Anyway? A Quick Overview of the Whole Bible, Mark Dever (2010)

The Church and the Surprising Offense of God's Love: Reintroducing the Doctrines of Church Membership and Discipline, Jonathan Leeman (2010)

What Is a Healthy Church Member?, Thabiti M. Anyabwile (2008)

12 Challenges Churches Face, Mark Dever (2008)

The Gospel and Personal Evangelism, Mark Dever (2007)

What Is a Healthy Church?, Mark Dever (2007)

ONE ASSEMBLY

Rethinking the Multisite and
Multiservice Church Models

Jonathan Leeman

WHEATON, ILLINOIS

Trade paperback ISBN: 978-1-4335-5959-4
ePub ISBN: 978-1-4335-5962-4
PDF ISBN: 978-1-4335-5960-0
Mobipocket ISBN: 978-1-4335-5961-7

Library of Congress Cataloging-in-Publication Data

Names: Leeman, Jonathan, 1973– author.
Title: One assembly: rethinking the multisite and multiservice church models / Jonathan Leeman.
Description: Wheaton, Illinois: Crossway, 2020. | Series: 9Marks | Includes bibliographical references and index.
Identifiers: LCCN 2019036101 | ISBN 9781433559594 (trade paperback) | ISBN 9781433559600 (pdf) | ISBN 9781433559617 (mobipocket) | ISBN 9781433559624 (epub)
Subjects: LCSH: Multi-site churches. | Church.
Classification: LCC BV637.95 .L44 2020 | DDC 254—dc23
LC record available at https://lccn.loc.gov/2019036101

Crossway is a publishing ministry of Good News Publishers.

LB		30	29	28	27	26	25	24	23	22	21	20
15	14	13	12	11	10	9	8	7	6	5	4	3	2	1

CONTENTS

SERIES PREFACE

The 9Marks series of books is premised on two basic ideas. First, the local church is far more important to the Christian life than many Christians today perhaps realize.

Second, local churches grow in life and vitality as they organize their lives around God's word. God speaks. Churches should listen and follow. It's that simple. When a church listens and follows, it begins to look like the One it is following. It reflects his love and holiness. It displays his glory. A church will look like him as it listens to him.

So our basic message to churches is, don't look to the best business practices or the latest styles; look to God. Start by listening to God's word again.

Out of this overall project comes the 9Marks series of books. Some target pastors. Some target church members. Hopefully all will combine careful biblical examination, theological reflection, cultural consideration, corporate application, and even a bit of individual exhortation. The best Christian books are always both theological and practical.

It's our prayer that God will use this volume and the others to help prepare his bride, the church, with radiance and splendor for the day of his coming.

SPECIAL THANKS

A number of friends read and offered good counsel on this book. So thank you, Alex Duke, Sam Emadi, Grant Gaines, Greg Gilbert, Bobby Jamieson, Michael Lawrence, Jake Meador, Aaron Menikoff, Anne Rabe, Matthew Sleeman, Matt Smethhurst, and Mark Vroegop. I'm also grateful to Mark Dever and Ryan Townsend for their support, encouragement, and feedback. Finally, Crossway—particularly Lane Dennis, Dave DeWit, and Thom Notaro—have been both patient and helpful every step of the way. Not all these names share my perspective, so don't blame them. But each contributed in love to make the book better.

INTRODUCTION

The church's main hall is full. People in the back scan the crowd, looking for an empty seat. You cannot see any. I am assisting a flustered usher. She is assisting a flustered mother with young children. Where can we put them?

Four young, single men sit comfortably in the back row. They're oblivious. I want to say something. Hello, guys?

These days you have to show up early if you want seats. It's the same upstairs on the children's ministry floor. Want to check your toddler into childcare during the service? Better get there fifteen minutes early. Even then, you'll find a crowd of parents hovering, waiting for check-in to begin.

Back downstairs with the big people, the usher runs out of bulletins. She panics. There's nothing else I can do. I sit down with my family. Oh well.

Another Sunday morning in a full church.

Multisite or Multiservice—An Easy and Wise Solution?

I'm not exaggerating, by the way. The very Sunday after I wrote the words above, I arrived twenty minutes early at the children's ministry check-in desk with my three-year-old. Her class was already full. I walked away quietly chuckling at the irony. "Are you sure you want to argue against multiple services or sites?" I asked myself. My daughter spent the entire service on my lap.

For moments like these, starting a second site or service does seem like the obvious solution. It seems like *good financial stewardship* because it's more cost-effective than building a bigger building. It seems like *good time stewardship* because it's less logistically taxing than planting a whole new church and can happen more quickly. It offers *predictability and familiarity* for church members and *pastoral safety* for leaders. You avoid sending forty vulnerable sheep off to start a new church with a young, untested planter.

Most crucially, it makes *Great Commission sense*. We want as many people as possible to hear the gospel. We don't want them leaving because they cannot find seats. Therefore, let's not be too persnickety over the structures of a church. Right? A number of good friends, whom I respect and who are better evangelists than I am, have chosen multisite or multiservice for just this reason.

Of course, not all reasons for adding sites or services commend themselves. One multisite pastor told his staff that becoming a multisite church made them appear "legitimate." It was a status symbol for him. But never mind the bad reasons. What do we make of the good reasons, like the Great Commission?

That's what motivated my pastor friend Mark to adopt the multisite model. He challenged me over dinner, "If a non-Christian walks into our church, and it's full, I cannot tell him to go elsewhere." He continued, "Suppose you have a revival, and an extra few hundred people show up one Sunday. Would you turn them away?" I hope not.

Another multisite pastor friend, J. D. Greear, wrote that the elders of his church chose to pursue a multisite strategy because they "believed it was the most efficient way to reach the maximum number of people in our city . . . as quickly as possible." J. D. well understands that a concern for evangelism does not negate everything else the Bible says about the church. He, too, values "accountability, community, and faithful polity." Yet, he maintains that "a church that does not have [evangelism] near the top of its priorities cannot be closely aligned with our Savior's purposes, regardless of what else they get right. In heaven, there is more joy over one sinner that repents than how we organize the 99 who are already his."[1] Insisting

DEFINING MULTISITE

Geoff Surratt, Greg Ligon, and Warren Bird's definition of a multisite church emphasizes the shared leadership and administrative structure: "A multi-site church shares a common vision, budget, leadership, and board."* John Piper's definition emphasizes the shared leadership and the teaching: "The essence of biblical church community and unity hangs on a unity of eldership, a unity of teaching, and a unity of philosophy of ministry."†

* Geoff Surratt, Greg Ligon, and Warren Bird, *The Multi-site Revolution: Being One Church . . . in Many Locations* (Grand Rapids, MI: Zondervan, 2006), 18.

† John Piper, "Is It Important for the Sake of Community That a Church Have Only One Service?," desiringGod.org, October 20, 2008, https://www.desiringgod.org/interviews/is-it-important-for-the-sake-of-community-that-a-church-have-only-one-service.

on the single-assembly church, J. D. contends, is "evangelistically harmful."

Both of these conversations illustrate the strength of Great Commission instincts among evangelicals. We recognize that salvation is most crucial. This is both a doctrinal conviction and an automatic reflex. Salvation is more important than goods and kindred, more important than the kingdoms of this world, and certainly more important than church order. As Martin Luther taught us to sing,

> Let goods and kindred go,
> this mortal life also;
> the body they may kill.

So, in one sense, I agree with Pastors Mark and J. D. entirely. We should prize conversion and spiritual growth over church structure. And the Great Commission should be uppermost in our minds as churches.

Might We Be Shortsighted?

But hold on. Should we pit church structure and conversion against one another? I care about my children more than my house, but my house keeps my children alive and healthy. Likewise, evangelicals rightly prioritize salvation, but we cannot abandon the house of salvation, which is the church. Doing so will hurt our ability to fulfill the Great Commission. It's true there is more joy over one sinner who repents than a rightly organized ninety-nine. Yet, let's not grab an *either–or* where the Bible provides a *both–and*. Jesus in fact uses this very illustration about the ninety-nine and the one just so: rightly organizing the ninety-nine is crucial for reaching the one (Matt. 18:10–20). Read the parable about the lost sheep in context.

As evangelicals, we can be shortsighted, like eating candy before a marathon for the burst of sugar energy we expect it to give. We fixate on the number of people in the pews *this Sunday*, but lose sight of how a healthy biblical church is the best way to fulfill the Great Commission over time—to run the whole marathon with endurance. Biblical church order serves disciple-making. Biblical polity aids evangelism. Don't separate them.

Too often, we are tempted to change the rules to get more of a good thing. Yet, in the process we undermine ourselves. Think of a university that addresses a downward trend in student grades by making tests easier. They might fix the grade problem in the short term, but they won't produce better engineers, nurses, or math teachers over time. Or think of a clothing company that increases profits by producing cheaper clothes. They'll do better in the short run, but they'll hurt their reputation in the long run. I stopped shopping at one of my favorite stores because holes in the sweaters and unstitched seams in the shirts showed up after one season of wearing them.

In the same way, the good desire for conversions shouldn't lead us to compromise other biblical principles. It will hurt those numbers and the church's mission in the long run. "A growing number of people is not a number of growing people," Mark Dever has said. Unbiblical methods and strategies for fulfilling the Great Commission might look good for a moment, like grade inflation ballooning the number of As. But they produce false positives, inaccurate readings, anemic churches, a weakened mission. They hinder the Great Commission. Healthy, biblical churches, on the other hand, advance it.

Those Sites and Services *Are* Churches

Which brings us back to the multisite and multiservice models. Here's the biggest problem, as I'll seek to show in this book: They're not in the Bible. At all. And that means they work against, not with, Jesus's disciple-making plan.

To put it another way: *there is no such thing as a multisite or multiservice church* based on how the Bible defines a church. They don't exist. Adding a second site or service, by the standards of Scripture, gives you two churches, not one. Two assemblies, separated by geography or numbers on a clock, give you two churches.

Plenty of things exist today that *call* themselves multisite or multiservice churches: "Join us on Sunday at 9:00 or 11:00," or "One church, three locations." Such a "church" might be a legal and institutional reality, and I will use the singular word "church" throughout this book when referring to a multisite or multiservice arrangement as a legal and institutional entity. But make no mistake, biblically speaking, such entities form a collection of churches. Each site and service is its own church, even as they share pastors, a budget, and a brand. The "north campus" and the "south campus" are both churches. The 9:00 a.m. service and the 11:00 a.m. service are both churches.

Jesus says, "Where two or three are gathered in my name, there am I among them" (Matt. 18:20). He's not "there" in the administrative structure that binds several campuses together. He's not "among" the unified vision, budget, and board. He's there in the gathering of two or three, or two or three thousand. The gathering represents him, speaks for him, flies his flag. If you want a proof text for this whole book, here it is in three present-in-time-and-

WHAT ABOUT THE DIFFERENCES BETWEEN SITES AND SERVICES?

A year before completing this book I gave a short talk on the topic of this book at a pastors' retreat, and several pastors were surprised that I equated multisite churches and multiservice churches. After the talk, one pastor said to me, "Multisite and multiservice are different kinds of things. Why are you lumping them together?"

I agree they are things we experience differently. Different impulses motivate a church to go in one direction or the other. And the different institutional configurations have different relational and logistical implications, which means the two configurations will differently impact a church's ability to fulfill its mission. That said, multisite and multiservice churches have this in common: they divide the assembly. One divides it geographically, the other chronologically, producing more than one assembly. And if I'm right that, formally speaking, the regular assembly is an essential ingredient for making a church a church, then both multiple sites and multiple services present us with multiple churches.

space words: "gather," "there," "among." Matthew 18:20 does not provide all the ingredients for a church, as we'll think about in chapter 1. The New Testament also adds preaching and the ordinances for specifying how we gather "in his name." Yet a church doesn't possess less than the ingredients mentioned here. It's not less than a gathering. Jesus is there at 9:00 a.m. He's there at 11:00. Each speaks for him. Each can act for him. Each is a church. And this is the uninterrupted pattern we'll discover throughout the New Testament regarding local churches.

It's common these days to say that a church is a people, not a place. And that's sort of true. It's the people who *are* a church—not the building, pastors, budget, vision, or brand. But those people *become* a church in part by gathering in a place. That place, that gathering, is the geography of Christ's kingdom, as I'll also argue in chapter 1. One might as well say, "A basketball team is a people, not a practice or a game." Again, true, but it misses something crucial. The players become a team by practicing and playing together. No practicing and playing as one, no team. For a church, likewise, a physical togetherness, an assembly, is an essential part of the formula.

When you read "church" in your English Bible, the Greek word behind it is *ekklēsia*, which, in the plainest translation, is "assembly."[2] Again, a New Testament church is more than an assembly, but it's not less, as I'll seek to show. A people who don't regularly assemble cannot be an assembly, a church. They're just a bunch of people. Meanwhile, contemplate the word "multisite." It means *sites multiple, not together, not an assembly.*

One friend told me he liked the idea of the whole church being together, but he was uncertain of "how much we should insist on this principle of being single service or site." Let's be clear, I replied. There is no explicit "moral principle" in the Bible saying churches should stick to one site or service. I'm not starting with that kind of moral claim. I am starting with an ontological or a descriptive claim, as in: no matter what you call it, the Bible would say you have actually started another church with that second site or service. The second gathering, whether separated by time or by space, simply *is* its own church.

Structural Conversations Are Moral Conversations

Now, that ontological claim comes with moral implications. The problem is bigger and more complex than what we name the thing, because changing a church structure changes its moral shape.

We evangelicals don't know how to talk or think about structures, so strong are our individualistic and anti-institutional biases. At most, we treat the idea of church structure as pragmatic

"CHURCH" NOT A DIRECT TRANSLATION OF *EKKLĒSIA*

Part of what confuses our understanding of what constitutes a church is the fact that our English word "church" doesn't actually derive from *ekklēsia*. It roots back in the Greek word *kyriakos* (an adjective for "of the Lord," *kyrios*) or *kyriakē* (*oikia*), referring to a house of the Lord, which was sometimes used for houses of worship after AD 300. This eventually passed on through to the proto-Germanic *kirika* to the Old English *cirice* to the Middle English *chirche* to our own "church." As such, our English word "church" has spent centuries, like a slow meandering river, picking up all kinds of flotsam and sediment, from the idea of a building to the idea of a hierarchical structure (e.g., Roman Catholic *Church*, Evangelical Lutheran *Church*). So our English Bibles use "church" to translate *ekklēsia*, but the English word bears a much broader, more complicated range of meaning and resonance. Where *ekklēsia* possessed the comparatively brick-like clarity of "assembly," "church" is a more elastic word, carrying two thousand years' worth of accumulated intuitions and associations. One of the first translators of the English Bible, William Tyndale, therefore translated *ekklēsia* as "congregation"—for example, "and apon this rocke I wyll bylde my congregacion." All of this is to say, when we hear "church" with our English ears, we hear a lot more than early Greeks heard whenever someone said *ekklēsia*.

and arbitrary, as if it were a separate thing from what the church itself is. "A church structured *this* way or *that* way is still a church," we assume. "And the Bible leaves us freedom for structuring it *this* way or *that* way."

That's a fair assumption for some things, like whether or not we have a Sunday school program or small group ministry or task-specific deacons or biweekly elder meetings. But when it comes to defining what a church is or its basic system of governance, that's not the case. The very existence of a church depends upon some structure, some way of organizing and binding individual Christians together. No structure, no church.

Furthermore, realize what a "structure" is: it's a collection of rules, or moral judgments, that bind and shape our relationship with other people. To become a father or husband, for instance, is to occupy a rule structure that comes with a set of responsibilities—duties—and a package of rights and wrongs.

Structural conversations, in other words, are moral conversations. That's true in every domain of life, whether home, work, or government. It's true in matters of church structure, too.

To the seminary ethics professors out there, you should teach church structure and polity in your ethics class, because that's what church polity is—one subcategory of ethics.

So back to my original point: change a church's structure and you change the moral shape of the church. You change how people relate—their sense of responsibility to one another—however subtly and imperceptibly. Changing from a congregational to a presbyterian or an episcopal church government, for instance, changes its moral shape. Each distributes responsibilities and duties between leaders and members differently. You give more responsibility to the leaders, less to the members. Likewise, changing from one service to two, or one site to three, does the same thing, even if people are not fully aware of those differences. Whether you mean to or not, you inevitably shift some degree of authority and responsibility upward onto the shoulders of the leaders, even if you maintain the same formal structure (congregational, elder-rule, etc.). Over time, that shift, like wheels aimed at a slightly new angle, will dramatically alter the direction of the church and how it fulfills its mission.

The question for Christians, therefore, must be Does the Bible say anything about church structure? Christian ethics must be biblical ethics. Where the Bible morally binds the conscience, we bind the conscience. Where it doesn't, we don't, but leave each believer to the realm of prudence and freedom. We want our ethics (or church structures) to depend not upon the wisdom of man but upon the inspired wisdom of God. We don't want our church structures to demand more than the Bible says, but nor do we want them to demand less than the Bible says.

In short, we all need two lists: a list of the structural things the Bible mandates for all churches everywhere because they make a church a church, and a list of the things that can vary from context to context. My concern in this book is with that first list. We want to define the church like Jesus defines the church; else we'll ask our churches to do different things than Jesus asks them to do. And that raises questions of faithfulness and obedience.

If Jesus points to an assembly and says, "That's a church," while we point to a collection of assemblies bound together under one administration and say, "And that's a church," recognize what we're doing. We are changing the definition of what a church is. What's more, we are giving at least some of the work that should belong to the assembly to the administration that binds the multiple assemblies together. For the leadership, that's an act of usurpation; for the members, abdication. And this is true whether you are a congregationalist like me or not. We are, then, saying we know better how to handle discipleship, witness, and mission than Jesus. We are picking a fight with Jesus!

The Gospel and Gospel Structures

Let me say one more thing about biblical church structures: they emerge from the gospel itself. They are not arbitrary or artificially stapled onto God's people. Rather, the gospel produces a social order, and that order shows itself in how we organize our churches. The organization or order in turn protects and promotes the gospel (see fig. 1).

The gospel and biblical church order do not work at cross purposes. They reinforce one another.

Figure 1. Gospel flow chart

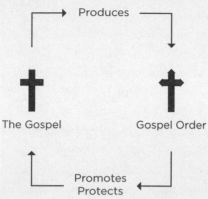

One of those biblical minimums of church order, this book is arguing, is one assembly. You can no more be a multisite church than you can be a multisite body. The single assembly of a church demonstrates, proves, embodies, illustrates, incarnates, makes concrete, makes palpable and touchable and hearable and seeable the unity we possess in the gospel. Gathering as a local assembly is the very first imperative to the indicative of the unity we possess as members of the universal church. It literally makes that unity visible and active. The body of Christ is not just an idea. Nor is the family of God. Nor is the temple of the Spirit. You can actually *see* and *hear* and *reach out and touch* the body, family, and temple in the gathering. The gathering manifests the universal church, or what people sometimes capitalize as the *Church*. The gathering makes the Church present, and a church present to itself. That is, it enables the members to discover, see, and recognize themselves together as *a* church and as *the* Church.

What's more, the gathering represents the authority of Christ. It depends upon and testifies to his lordship. Multisite advocates argue that once a church reaches a certain size, people cannot possibly know one another. This misses the point. A church is a church not because everyone knows everyone else, though we certainly hope everyone knows some people. A church is a church ultimately because of the authority of Christ and his declaration that he would identify himself with gatherings: "I'm there in the gathering of two or three in my name." That was his decision, not ours. Consider, therefore, what a church gathering is: it's a group of people bowed in submission to something. To what? To Christ. Their physical togetherness, then, testifies to his lordship.

Yet, divide the assembly in space or time, and gospel authority must move, once again, to the leaders who bind those assemblies together. The shared submission of those assemblies now testifies—again, even subtly—to the leaders who unite them.

It's therefore crucial to keep presence and authority tied together—both because Christ explicitly tied his name to the gathering and because he makes every member of the church a priest-king. Presence and authority are in sync in the assembly.

That said, there's an inevitability to the authority of Jesus in the gathering. A friend in a doctrinally solid multisite church recently told me their members' meetings, which combine all the campuses, are in a downward spiral of conflict. Members of the three sites each prefer the leadership of their own campus pastors and find themselves tempted to mistrust the pastors from other campuses. It's true their conflict might have had a number of sources, but the thought bubble above my head read, "You have separated presence and authority and gone against the biblical pattern. You picked a fight with Jesus. I'm sad, but not surprised by the resulting tensions."

Church Intuitions

Let me explain our fight with Jesus one more way. We all have a basic set of intuitions about what a church is. An intuition, mind you, is your gut sense about something, your snap judgment about it before you consciously think about it. And we all have a gut sense about what a church is, an automatic reflex that shows up in the way we talk about a church.

Suppose you reflexively think of the church as a building. You will talk about "driving down to the church" or "walking inside the church." You'll exclaim, "I can't believe they're selling the church to a condo developer." Or you might view a church as a performance event, like a show or a concert. You "enjoyed church yesterday." You "are frustrated by how long church lasted." Or you might view a "church" as its leaders. You "love the church's vision." You "heard the church excommunicated Jack" or "the church changed its doctrine," by which you mean the pastors did those things.

In each of these scenarios, whatever your doctrine is, your intuitive or functional view determines your practice.

To be sure, our church intuitions can be more or less biblical, mixing biblical elements together with cultural elements. And they can change over time. I expect that some of my intuitions are misshaped. Admittedly, it's hard to see which ones. If you want to know about the water, don't ask the fish. But compare the phrases mentioned above about "driving down to the church" or "enjoying church" with the way the Bible uses the word.

The Bible talks about the church *as a people*.

- "Tell it to the church" (Matt. 18:17).
- "When he had landed at Caesarea, he went up and greeted the *church*, and then went down to Antioch" (Acts 18:22).
- "Greet also the *church* in their house" (Rom. 16:5).

It talks about it *as a people who gather together*.

- "And when they arrived and gathered the *church* together, they declared all that God had done with them" (Acts 14:27).
- "When you come together as a *church*, I hear that there are divisions among you. . . . So then, my brothers, when you come together to eat, wait for one another" (1 Cor. 11:18, 33).
- "If, therefore, the whole *church* comes together and all speak in tongues . . ." (1 Cor. 14:23).

It talks about the church *as a people who act together*.

- "And if they refuse to listen even to the *church* . . ." (Matt. 18:17).

- "When they came to Jerusalem, they were welcomed by the *church*. . . . Then it seemed good to the apostles and elders, with the whole *church*, to choose men from among them and send them" (Acts 15:4, 22).

Notice that this last example also distinguished the church from the leaders.

I'm not suggesting verses like these are proof of one assembly. My point is merely that these biblical authors talk about the church a little differently than we do.

Furthermore, if your idea of a church at the functional or gut level is *a building*, you will do quite a bit to take care of that building. The building will be very important to you. If your view at the functional or gut level is *performance*, you will prioritize attending the performance and the quality of the performance, but you might not prioritize your participation in worship and spending time with the church family the rest of the week.

The fight with Jesus, then, shows up in any area where our view of the church differs from his. The person who intuitively or functionally views the church as a weekly performance will more likely attend to some biblical duties but not others. We fight Jesus by redefining the church. We fight Jesus by forsaking any of the responsibilities he's given to us.

If this book were a full-on ecclesiology, we would have to talk about the church as family, church as body, church as bride, church as pillar and foundation of truth, church as citizens of the kingdom, and so forth. We would need both the structural, institutional elements and the familial, fellowship elements—the skeleton and the muscle. And we would need to ensure that our intuitive assumptions and sense of responsibility were stuffed full with all that wonderful content.

The single biblical element we're meditating upon in this book comes from the word itself—*ekklēsia* in the Greek, "church" in English. Have you ever stopped and asked why Jesus picked the word *ekklēsia*? He could have used a more religious-sounding word like "synagogue." We would have advised him to use softer, more inclusive words like "community" or "fellowship" or "society." And certainly, he and the apostles were happy to use other metaphors, too, like "flock" and "family" and "body." But Jesus also chose a hard-boundary, brick-heavy word that to first-century ears meant "assembly," whether people were reading the Greek Old Testament or classical Greek writers like Aristotle. They would have heard it with different intuitions or assumptions than we possess when we hear the word "church." It's a religious word for us. For them it was more political. It communicates *building* to us, not to them. It insinuates a *hierarchy* to us, not to them.

Turning back to the topic of multisite and multiservice models, then, realize that our ability to make sense of these models depends not just upon our formal doctrine but also upon our intuitions. If you intuitively view the church as a building, you won't balk when the pastors recommend adding a second service. Same building, same church, right? If you intuitively view the church as a Sunday morning performance or as the leadership, you won't think it's weird when they recommend adding another site. It won't violate your sense of what the church is or needs. In fact, why not perform this show in as many venues as possible?

Marketplace Intuitions

Think about it. Through the centuries, Christians have often built churches mimicking the structures of the culture around them. The Roman pope and episcopacy of the 600s matched itself to the Roman emperor and hierarchies of the Roman government. The committee structures of Baptist churches in America in the 1950s matched themselves to the corporate structures of the General Electric and Ford Motor Company of the 1950s. And churches in Africa today often treat the pastor like a tribal chief. The lesson is that none of us should assume we are impervious to our surrounding influences.

Multisite or multiservice pastor friends of mine have admitted they adopted the model without first doing a careful study. The literature says the same. "Without really thinking about it, we became a multi-site and video-venue church," says Mark Driscoll.[3] Brad House and Gregg Allison testify to the point more broadly: "Multisite leaders are fond of borrowing a phrase from startup companies that boast about 'building the plane in the air.'"[4]

Now, leading and growing an organization always involve some improvisation. Yet consider what people do when they improvise. They look around the room to see what's lying about, what objects or words or ideas can be put to use. Is it any surprise, therefore, that in the last fifty years American churches would pursue the multiple-site-and-service model? When we are not "really thinking about it," we inevitably stray in the direction of what's already around us.

Our intuitions are swayed by the marketplace more than we care to admit. If you lived through the 1970s to '90s, you witnessed the larger chains swallowing up all the independent retailers. You remember when Barnes & Noble closed down your favorite bookstore, Blockbuster Video shuttered the local video shop, and Jiffy Lubes began popping up on the corners where the independent garages used to sit. By the same token, you might remember when small churches kept closing their doors at approximately the same rate that the nearby megachurch was building yet another addition.[5] As Ed Stetzer has noted, "There are as many megachurches today in the greater Nashville area as there were in the entire country in 1960." Multiservice churches existed before the 1970s, but they started to become commonplace through the 1980s and '90s, reaching 32 percent of churches by 2016.[6] In 1990 ten churches nationwide were multisite; in 2019 over five thousand were.[7]

In the twenty-first century, we have watched the aforementioned chain retailers lose to the Internet: Barnes & Noble has given way to Amazon; Blockbuster Video to Netflix. Times change. Sure enough, the Internet church becomes a thing. Well-known churches like

Saddleback, Life.Church, Northpoint, and others all offer "online campuses." If you accept the premise of multisite, in which *gathering* and *church* are unlinked, it's hard to dispute the logic of the Internet church. Unhooking the word "church" from a gathering of one people (multiservice) and a geographic location (multisite) makes this the next logical step. The word "multisite," again, justifies the phenomena—why not have as many sites as there are members?

And the trend continues. One writer recently praised something he called the "omni-channel approach." This allows members to "attend one Sunday, listen to the message on podcast the following week, watch a live online stream the Sunday after, and catch the message on-demand in an church app the week after that." The point is, he said, we're shifting from "a location-centric approach, to an audience-centric approach."[8]

This is the era of the franchise, the celebrity, quality entertainment, and the Internet. We value quality products, quick access, efficient processes, predictable outcomes, and visible results. From governments to schools to churches, we want our leaders to provide the answers and to do all the work. In this environment, the multisite and multiservice models simply make sense. They're intuitive.

And please understand: I'm not just pointing the finger. I can complain about the closing of bookstores in one minute and order a book from Amazon in the next; critique consumerism in churches in my weekday job, and then complain in my heart about the music on Sunday. I distinctly remember showing up once in a small church where the only instrument was a pianist banging out the basic chords of the hymns we sang. His lack of skill distracted me. Like most people, I like entertainment-production quality, including in my church.

In such a world, to oppose multiple sites and services can feel like opposing the Internet. Good luck. Church leaders concede these models are "not ideal," like "not baking your own bread is not ideal." So we shrug our shoulders and resign ourselves to the fact that this is how the world works nowadays.

When I told one pastor friend I was writing this book, he replied, "People are going to think you're a loon!" I remember because I don't hear the word "loon" very often. Yet I think he's right. Conversation after conversation tells me this book is spitting into the wind. Why? Either because I'm wrong, which is possible, or because the multisite and multiservice models accord with today's cultural intuitions, of which I'm certain. The multisite and multiservice models feel like "Of course!" and "Why not!" which tells you that our intuitions are speaking. Franchise restaurants, movie theaters, voluntary associations, consumeristic mentalities, our obsession with celebrities and political leaders, autonomy and personal choice, professional-quality media productions, growing expectations of big government, brand management and consistency—all this provides the soil in which multiple sites and services naturally sprout, particularly when we are "not really thinking about it." Then, if we are challenged to think about it, we want to defend what we've already built.

Therefore, I'm asking you to do two things as you read this book. First, consider the biblical arguments. But, second, stop and examine your own intuitions or assumptions about what a church is. Could they be less biblical and more contemporary than you realize?

Subtly Changing Intuitions

I am not saying the members and leaders of multisite and multiservice churches are all consumers. Many preach against consumerism. Multisite pastor Mark Driscoll argues that "a campus is not set up for church consumers" and that approaching church like consumers "is sin."[9]

The trouble is that the institutional structures speak and teach and train. The medium is the message, as it's said. And the multiple-site-and-service structure works against the best pastoral intentions. The "church" is no longer just the gathered people. The "church" is now several gatherings of people, plus the administrative superstructure. So guess where the burden of responsibility shifts? To the thing uniting all those groups of people—the administrative superstructure, which includes the leaders and their weekly performance.

Compare the experience of stepping into three different churches.

Multiservice

Let's start at the 9:00 a.m. service of a multiservice church. A pastor stands up and welcomes everyone to "Redemption Church." What or who is Redemption Church? Well, our doctrine tells us that Redemption Church is a people, not a place. So Redemption Church, on paper, must be the members in the building at the moment, together with the members who show up at the 10:30 and noon services—everyone who signed a membership covenant. The thing is, no one gets to sing or pray or hear sermons with "the church." The only shared experience "the church" enjoys is the building and the performance, albeit at different times; like "You saw the Broadway show Hamilton? So did I!" The shared building and performance, experientially, makes the church a "we" and an "us."

Church ends. We head to a restaurant. We bump into another member from the church and say, "Did you make it to church?" or "Wasn't church great?" By "make it to church," we don't mean all the members, in spite of our theology, because the members never actually met as one. We mean the people up front or the building. "Wasn't church great," too, means the people up front. The people up front are what we all shared. The membership (church) didn't do anything together.

The same verbal ambiguity occurs later in the week when we invite our non-Christian neighbors to "church," meaning the event or performance at the 9:00 or 10:30 or noon hour. We cannot invite them to the actual church itself, that is, the members, because the church (the members) never meets.

And little by little our church intuitions change. In the way we use the word "church," and talk about "church," and think about what "church" is, "church" changes from a people to a performance or leaders or a building, even if our doctrine stays the same. We don't treat it like Scripture does: "Greet also the *church* in their house" (Rom. 16:5); "Then it seemed good to the apostles and elders, with the whole *church*, to choose men from among them" (Acts. 15:22).

This doesn't just happen among consumeristic, megachurch Americans. It can happen anywhere. I asked a bus tour driver in Kenya if he had a church. "Yes." What kind of church is it? "Anglican." Do you like your church? "Yes." How come? "Because if I miss one service, I can just attend another one." I dare surmise, the mere fact that his church had multiple services— no matter what else may or may not be true about his church—worked against his ability to apprehend his church as a people to whom and for whom he is responsible.

One Assembly

Suppose then we leave Redemption Church and attend the single weekly gathering of Faith Church. The pastor there also refers to "our church" and "Christ's body" and "the family of God." But now those words mean something touchable, hearable, seeable. We can look around the room and behold with our eyes the "family" and "body" of Faith Church. The universal church is fully manifest in that room, where the temperature rises by seven degrees from the body heat. Faith Church is united by the people up front, as in the multiservice Redemption Church. But it's also united by its own performance. Together the church sings and the church prays and the church listens and the church makes decisions, even if five thousand people are in the room. And it's this shared performance of all the people, gathered in Jesus's name through preaching and the Supper in one place, that makes Faith Church a church, a fam-

DON'T MULTISITE CHURCHES COME IN A VARIETY OF MODELS?

Multisite churches come in all sorts of shapes and sizes. Some project the preacher on a screen. Some ask him to speed across town by car to preach in each location. Some have their own campus pastors who do the work or split the work of preaching. Some gather every campus together quarterly. Some permit each campus to exercise a degree of autonomy; some don't. I'm not going to work through all these differences example by example, and I happily admit that some formulations better conform to the scriptural pattern than others.

The common denominator I'm interested in is with anything that calls itself a "church" but has more than one weekly gathering comprising different sets of individuals. (I'm not speaking about a church that has, say, a morning and an evening service, where the same people attend both services.)

ily, a body. Ironically, Redemption "Church" can never do these things as a church.

Two different structures cultivate two sets of intuitions over time.

Multisite

Now, let's travel over to a third church, the multisite Grace Church. I'm not surprised that the multiservice church became commonplace in the American church experience before the multisite did. Multiservice *feels* less troubling to the oneness and "churchness" of a church. Members of the multiservice all gather in the same building. They see each other in the hallways and parking lot. At the same time, the multiservice model broke the connection between church and gathering. It trained Christians to view "church" as performance for several decades, allowing the multisite model to easily, perhaps inevitably, follow, just like the Internet church inevitably follows the multisite church. That said, ironically, some multisite models do better than others, as well as better than the multiservice model, at teaching people that the church involves gathering. Members of a campus or site will sometimes possess their own space, their own pastors, their own music leaders, and sometimes even their own preacher, and often (most crucially) a stable group of members. Relative to the members of any given *service*, therefore, the members of any given *site* will potentially cultivate a thicker sense of "we."

That said, the "church" remains one head with multiple bodies. So we show up at the south campus of Grace Church. When the service leader refers to "our church," "this body," and "this family," these concepts remain as abstract and non-incarnate as in the multiservice Redemption Church. Then the preacher appears on video. He might be in the most dangerous place of all, so much prominence being given to him. Each site has its own band and dedicated pastors, but this charismatic and gifted communicator is the primary point of ecclesiastical and structural unity between different campuses. He is the only human being that everyone in all the sites and services encounters in common. He is the pinnacle and essence of what makes a video-model multisite church a church. It's almost as if the church finds its identity in him. The church is a "we" through him. Despite the best intentions, the church becomes the church of *that preacher*. It's identified with him. It draws visitors through him. Members have dinner and talk about him. He is the source of every member's pleasure or displeasure, and the subject of newspaper articles. The members know well enough to say with their mouths that the church is the people. But functionally, the church is identified with him. Again, our intuitions change, even when our doctrine doesn't.

To be sure, this emphasis on a superstar pastor can occur at a one-assembly church, too. But the structures of the multisite church require it, because he quite literally *is* the point and substance of unity between campuses. He is therefore at the very core of what constitutes Grace "Church."

In short, change the basic biblical structures and you'll slowly, subtly change people's understanding of what the church is, what the church does, and what members are responsible to do.

My pastor friend Bob learned all this the hard way. When he led the church from three services back to one, he discovered how the very fact of three services had taught the church poorly. Here's how Bob put it:

> Years ago, we outgrew our space, so we added a second service, and then a third. The result was that I was teaching my people that their church provided options for them that they could select for what suited them on that day. Up too late on Saturday night? No problem, pick the late service. Got a lot to do on Sunday? No problem, hit the early service. It's not that I ever said that, but that is what happened. In fact, over time the people who came to the early service were so committed to the convenience of that time, that when we were able to all meet together at one time in one place, they left. I only thought they were part of the church. Initially, I wanted to blame them for thinking only of themselves and not being committed. Then it dawned on me. I had taught them that.[10]

If the church is a family that gathers, what might seem like a subtle structural alteration—going from one service to two then three—changes the DNA of what a church is. It's now not a family that gathers but an event to attend or the people up front. And that mutation will teach, even if you teach with your mouth contrariwise. The medium is the message.

Conclusion

You want the argument of this book in a nutshell? I'll give it to you in three r's: Multisite and multiservice churches *repudiate* the Bible's definition of a church, *redefine* what a church is, and so *reshape* the church morally. And all that means these models pick a fight with Jesus. The fight involves abdication by the members and usurpation by the leaders, even if unintended.

Think back to the gospel flow chart above (p. 23). By changing what a church is, the multiple-site-and-service model, like unbiblical polity in general, subtly

- weakens a church's ability to protect both the gospel and the people of the gospel,
- puts the pastors in a spiritually precarious position,
- weakens every member's individual Christian discipleship, and
- hurts evangelism and the church's witness.

I keep saying "subtle" or "subtly," just like the sinking foundation under my last home was subtle. It took a decade for the crack in the wall and ceiling to widen to the point where we could identify the problem. So, too, the weakened foundations of a multisite or multiservice church show themselves only over time, sometimes decades.

Good pastors in multisite and multiservice churches have an instinctive sense of these problems and therefore will work against the ill effects of the changes. I can name dozens of otherwise healthy multisite and multiservice churches filled with good Christians doing great work. But the change in what the church *is* is real because it's mathematically hardwired into the structure: two is not one. And these pastors and churches will always have to work against their structure, like running on a track with weights around your legs. Over time, furthermore, people will easily lose sight of their every-member responsibilities and corporate purposes.

For all these reasons and more, it is by no means clear to me that multisite and multiservice churches will do a better job of reaching

PICKING A FIGHT WITH JESUS? REALLY?

A multisite pastor friend of mine graciously read a draft of this book. Amid affirming comments, he also observed, "I don't like this 'fight with Jesus' thing—at all." How serious a charge was I making? he wondered. "Where does multisite fall on the theological triage scale?"

The phrase "theological triage" refers to how important a doctrine is, the way an emergency room nurse has to triage patients coming through the door. *First-order doctrines* are essential to the gospel. Think of the Trinity, the doctrine of sin, or Christ's person and work. Get them wrong and you get the gospel wrong.

Matters of church definition as well as church organization such as baptism, the Supper, and polity are *second-order doctrines*. If first-order doctrines are essential to the gospel, second-order issues are important for protecting the gospel over time. Plus, they are essential to being a church, because that's one thing a church does—protect the gospel over time. Baptists and Presbyterians can agree on first-order issues and so affirm one another as Christians. But they define the church differently. Baptists like me define a church as "believers." Presbyterians define it as "believers and their children."

Third-order doctrines are issues we can disagree on but still be members of the same church, like our view on the millennium or the gift of tongues.

The multisite question, I believe, is a second-order question. It concerns a new definition of a church: multiple gatherings and their administrative superstructure. For that reason, my regard for multisiters matches my regard for Presbyterians. I happily embrace each in the gospel, but with hat in hand and love in my heart, yes, I believe that both pick a fight with Jesus by wrongly defining the church.

the lost. Even while the numbers of the multisite megachurches explode, let's remember, we do not have heaven's eyes. Tabulating conversions is not like counting widgets rolling down the assembly line. I therefore don't assume that, on the last day, when the real numbers are tallied, multisite methods will prove to be "the most efficient way to reach the maximum number of people as quickly as possible," at least if they are building on the wisdom of man instead of God.

I think of my pastor friend Paul who added a second service to his church when the building became full. His motives were good: he didn't want to close the doors to unbelievers. Yet he was also cautious about dividing the church. "We were completely committed to remaining one church," he told me. Therefore, he led the church to adopt every measure they could think of to maintain that sense of oneness. "I was determined it would work," he continued. "Every elder committed to be at both services. The services were identical in every way, and we put a fellowship time between the services." They asked people in the first service to stay late and people in the second to come early.

Yet, after ten months of trying hard, Paul said, "We realized we were creating two churches." New members didn't know people in the other service. And the Spirit did different things in the two services, even as the leaders tried to keep them identical. The two assemblies simply encountered different experiences, and "two services made us two churches." Plus, each church was a little weaker because of the model. Members relied more on the elders to maintain the sense of unity. And the elders were effectively pastoring two churches, meaning there was less of them for each. There was an unintended abdication and usurpation.

Therefore, they "squished" (Paul's word) everyone back into one service. The first Sunday back together, Paul said, was a mix of joy ("so good to be here with you again") and surprise ("you've been coming to the church for *how* long?"). Eventually, they found a bigger meeting space. Not only that, a nearby church needed help. So they sent a pastor and thirty members, reigniting that congregation and its witness.

What they learned in hindsight was that the pressure of a full building forced them to grow in ways they weren't expecting. At first, they thought about just themselves: how can *we* keep growing? The second service offered a pressure-release valve, which allowed them to remain parochial-minded and focused on their own ministry. Gratefully, they quickly realized this first solution created new problems. So they thought again: "Can we help other churches?" It would take sacrifice, but they discovered they could. Not only that, but they remembered that this other church is on the same team. By virtue of the gospel, the *we* includes *them* (the other church).

In short, defining the church the way Jesus defined the church, in spite of practical pressures to do otherwise, led to both spiritual and evangelistic growth. It forced them to become more catholic-minded, as I'll define that in chapter 3. And it gave them the opportunity to raise up another gospel witness, another church.

In fact, my map for this book starts there at the destination—chapter 3. Part of me wants you to begin there. The third chapter offers the alternative to multiple sites and services, and the alternative is exciting. Picture powerfully evangelistic churches working together, like you see in the New Testament; churches who think bigger than just their own ministries. That's the vision we need, and getting there requires us to nudge our church intuitions back in a catholic (small *c*) direction—meaning that the church is global, and we need to learn how to work together.

The alternative, in other words, is not a quick fix. It means changing the way we think—even feel—about "church" and our lives together in churches. Chapter 1 begins this process of reorientation by considering the kingdom theme in Scripture and why Jesus would use the word *ekklēsia*. I will call this gathering "the geography of Christ's kingdom." This chapter is the heaviest lift theologically.

Chapter 2 is basically one big word study on how the New Testament uses the word *ekklēsia*. I'll argue that, in spite of what you may have read elsewhere, the Bible consistently and uniformly presents local churches as assemblies.

Chapter 3, as I say, then points to the alternative, which is a far bigger church world than the one you might presently inhabit.

Ultimately, if we're going to know what to do when the building is so full the usher cannot find people seats, we need a different set of intuitions, intuitions that are more like Christ's and the apostles'. I hope that, even if you aren't finally persuaded by my exegesis, you'll enjoy meditating on the Bible and the church. That's what I try to do.

1

A CHURCH IS THE GEOGRAPHY
OF CHRIST'S KINGDOM

In the introduction, I argued that all of us view our churches through intuitions that are both biblical and cultural. My goal in this chapter is to pick up the kingdom theme in Scripture in order to push our church intuitions in a more political direction.

Maybe that sounds counterintuitive? But, no, I don't mean anything about Republicans and Democrats, lobbyists and legislatures. I mean that the gathering of a local church is an outpost or embassy of heaven. Through preaching and the ordinances, Jesus publicly identifies himself with us in the gatherings: "I am there among them," he said. He tied his authority to the gatherings. So it's there that we affirm our allegiance to him and our accountability to one another. There we raise his flag and brandish our kingdom passports. There his *ekklēsia* shows itself as an *ekklēsia* and acts as an *ekklēsia*.

In a sentence, the point of this chapter is this: the church gathering is where Christ's kingdom becomes visible and active, and Jesus's word *ekklēsia* communicates just this. By "visible" I mean you can literally see it, hear it, touch it. By "active" I mean we officially and publicly speak for the kingdom's sake. We conduct the kingdom's corporate business. Worship and submission unite.

Or let me put it this way: the church gathering is the "geography" of Christ's kingdom. Christians often say the church is not like ancient Israel in that it has no land, no geography. But the gathering is that geography. You might have visited an overseas embassy of your nation and heard it said that you were stepping onto the soil of your nation. The church gathering is where the nations of the earth can step inside the kingdom of heaven, this embassy of the eschaton. And it's where the citizens of that kingdom wield authority.

What Makes a Church a Church?

Let's start with the question What makes a church a church?

The married couple Oleg and Marina, brand-new believers, knew they wanted a church. They had learned the gospel from an American missionary named Will, yet there was no evangelical Protestant church in their twenty-thousand-person city in the Ural Mountains of Russia.

"Lord, give us a church in our city," they prayed.

One day in the market, Oleg and Marina met a watch repairman named Sergei. He had been in prison for stealing, but now the seventy-year-old man was a Christian. So was his wife, Zena, who had been a hardened atheist until her husband shared the gospel with her. Oleg and Marina noticed how Sergei used words like "God," "blessing," and "prayers." Finally, Marina asked, "Are you a Christian?" When Sergei said he was, she responded, "So are we! And we have been praying to find more believers in order to have a church." Sergei replied, "You must have been, because three days ago I prayed the same thing."

Marina asked Will to teach her and Oleg, Sergei and Zena, and their single friend Olga—five in all. They met on the second floor of Sergei's house, above the kitchen, in a room that serves as a bedroom and living room. For seven weeks Will explained the necessity of gospel belief, apostolic teaching, fellowship and accountability, the Lord's Supper, prayer, service, giving, worship, and evangelism. He taught about the church from Matthew 18 and Acts 2. He then asked the group of five, "Will you commit to these things together?" Oleg replied, "Except for the Lord's Supper we already do these things." The five of them split up a loaf of freshly baked white bread and ate it. Then they passed around a cup. Each drank.

They were now a church. They gave themselves the name "Christ's Church." All this happened four years ago (as of this writing), and since then more family members and friends have come to faith and joined.

From week one, they were a multiethnic, multinational church, including Udmurts, Russians, and Americans (Will and his wife). Now Ukrainians and a Tatar also belong to their number.

Traditional Protestant Answers

Back, then, to our question: What made Oleg, Marina, Sergei, Zena, Olga, and Will and his wife a church?

Before we look to Scripture ourselves, let's consider how Protestants before us, themselves drawing from Scripture, answered that question:

- *Lutherans.* "A congregation of saints in which the gospel is rightly taught and the Sacraments are rightly administered" (Augsburg Confession, art. 7).
- *Anglicans.* "A congregation of faithful men in which the pure Word of God is preached and the sacraments be duly ministered" (Thirty-Nine Articles, art. 19).
- *Presbyterians.* "Those . . . that profess true religion; and . . . their children" in "particular churches, which are . . . more or less pure, according as the doctrine of the gospel is taught and embraced, ordinances administered, and public worship performed" (Westminster Confession of Faith, 25.2, 4).
- *Baptists.* "A company of visible saints, called and separated from the world, by the Word and the Spirit of God, to the visible profession of the faith of the gospel, being baptized into the faith, and joined to the Lord, and each other, by mutual

agreement, in the practical enjoyment of the ordinances" (1644 London Baptist Confession, art. 33).

Drawing from these definitions, we might say that Marina, Oleg, Sergei, and the rest became a church by gathering together for certain activities, namely, preaching and the ordinances. The church isn't the activities; it's the people ("congregation," "company") as constituted by certain activities (preaching, ordinances). Further, we would say that Marina and company remain "a church" even when they are not engaged in those activities.[1]

The dynamic here is reminiscent of what makes a team a team. A team is a group of people who play a sport together, but not only *when* they play the sport together. You wouldn't call them a team if they never played as one. But insofar as they do, you would call them a team even when they are not together.[2] The function creates the thing, without which there is no thing.

Citizens of a Heavenly Kingdom

What these older definitions addressed only implicitly, however, is the question of location or the gathering. The gathering was assumed. There were no video campuses requiring these early Protestants to tighten up that part of their definitions.

But can we delocalize what these confessions say a local or particular church is? My short answer in this chapter is no. Jesus explicitly identifies himself with the gathering because the gathering makes his kingdom visible and active through their mutual agreement and testimony. The gathering, as I've said, is the "geography" of the kingdom.

To see that, let's imagine Oleg and the other six under an X-ray machine that gives us a biblical perspective on the skeletal structure holding them together as a particular church. What would we see?

Among other things, we would discover that, through the gospel, these seven are held together as citizens of Christ's kingdom. Their passports might say Udmurt, Russian, and American. Yet God delivered each of them "to the kingdom of his beloved Son" (Col. 1:13) and made them "fellow citizens" of this more ultimate nation (Eph. 2:19; also, Phil. 3:20). As such, their gatherings, set there in Russia's Ural Mountains, are like outposts or embassies of this heavenly kingdom.

Perhaps you are wondering, doesn't Christ's kingdom rule unite all Christians everywhere? Yes, it does: invisibly. What a local church does is make that rule visible. It expresses or manifests his kingdom rule in a way that everyone—insiders and outsiders—can actually see with their eyes and hear with their ears. This happens when a group of Christians physically gathers together, agrees upon the gospel to be preached, undertakes a naming ceremony (baptism), and then enjoys a regular family meal that affirms both the gospel and their unity (the Lord's Supper).

We need the biblical X-ray machine to see this because, entering that second-floor room, we don't *see* a kingdom, at least in terms that people typically associate with kingdoms. There are no flags, no government officials, no parliamentary buildings, no border entry stations. We only see this group of seven people doing what folk today call "religious" stuff.

Yet the biblical story of our church gatherings is set within the larger story of God's kingdom and how God reveals his rule on earth. God walked with Adam and Eve in the garden, a King in his kingdom. His rule was public and visible, both in his own person and in their obedience. When God excommunicated Adam and Eve from the garden for their sin, God remained King over all creation, yet his rule became invisible.

The course of redemptive history and geography in the Bible is the story of God making his rule and kingdom visible at different times in different ways. (Picture a submarine surfacing from time to time while crossing the Atlantic.) God publicly expressed his kingdom rule in mighty acts of judgment and salvation, covenantal institutions like the temple, and covenantal signs like circumcision. Most interesting for our purposes here, God also made his kingdom visible in the gatherings of his people. The Old Testament refers to these as "the assembly of the Lord" and "the assembly of Israel," and by the phrase "the day of the assembly." We'll come back to these in a moment.

Yet the story of the Old Testament is also the story of how inadequately the visible mechanisms of rule guide the human heart, which is desperately sick (Jer. 17:9). God therefore promised a new covenant, one that would establish his kingdom internally through the preaching of the gospel.

The new covenant, then, does its work, in the first instance, *invisibly*. The King forgives sins, giving every citizen of the covenant equal political standing before his throne. Then he writes his law on their hearts, so that every citizen will freely choose to obey (Jer. 31:31–34; Ezek. 36:24–27). Word and Spirit conspire together to produce a kingdom where the law is just and people want to obey it (Ezek. 37:1–14).

Meditate for just a moment on that: laws and hearts match! It's the greatest political program in history. It's the promise of the kingdom of heaven on earth.

The reforming of our church intuitions must begin here. There's a place to talk about other biblical metaphors, too, like body and family. But the political element is also central to what the church is. It's a skeletal structure, holding the whole thing together.

Making the Kingdom of Heaven Visible

Yet something is still missing from our new covenant storyline. This new covenant kingdom remains invisible, publicly inaccessible, unidentified. How does one citizen know who the others are? And how do the unbelieving nations know who does and does not belong to this kingdom? Members of the old covenant had circumcision, Sabbath keeping, and eventually a land to identify themselves, to say nothing of their familial and ethnic ties. Crucially, they also had "the assembly [*ekklēsia*] of the Lord" and "the day of the assembly." Yet what do the people of the new covenant have?

Or we could put the problem this way: the new covenant kingdom works from the inside out, unlike all other kingdoms and political communities, which work from the outside in. But the external trappings of a kingdom, for now, are suspended. There are no borders, land, government offices, flags, army, police force. Yet it's still a kingdom. So how do you exercise border patrol in a kingdom with no borders and no land? *Something* needs to make the very real, made-in-heaven political community of the new covenant visible.

Here we come to Jesus's presentation of the church. The church is not a shopper's club or exercise class, where we come once a week to get a good workout. The gathered, assembled, congregated church is the kingdom of heaven made visible on planet earth. It's Christians bound together—experiencing the firstfruits, the first taste, the first experience of God's society-creating rule.[3]

Walk to the second floor of Sergei's house and peek your head through the door when the seven Christians meet. Look, there it is! The kingdom of heaven in the gathered members of the church.

As I suggested a moment ago, the force field of God's rule binds all the saints both to him and to one another. We are all "fellow citizens" (Eph. 2:19). Yet that rule *manifests itself, enacts itself,* and *becomes visible* in the local assembly.[4] The kingdom of God becomes present in every particular congregation. How? The particular congregation or local church is where a group of saints both gather together and "shake hands" on the gospel (through the preaching and ordinances). It's where they agree on who Jesus is and that they are fellow disciples of Jesus, an agreement I will characterize as the essence of church authority in a moment.

When Christians formally gather together in Christ's name, they become the "geography" of Christ's presently landless kingdom. You can literally see it with your eyes because the people are gathered together. The gathering is like the US embassy in London. Walk inside, and they will tell you that you are standing on American soil. In a church that meets at different times or in different locations, you cannot do this. You cannot see "the church" (by their definition). You can only see a part of the church.

This is what Jesus says in Matthew's Gospel, especially chapters 16, 18, 26, and 28. We need to walk through these verses carefully, perhaps more painstakingly than anywhere else in the book. But right here is where I hope to prove from Scripture everything I've just said: Christ's kingdom rule becomes visible in the local church, and the demonstration of that kingdom rule requires a gathering where the saints affirm one another in the gospel and one another's membership in the gospel. Again, all this is part of reprogramming our church intuitions.

Are you ready?

Introducing the *Ekklēsia*

Jesus enters Matthew's Gospel telling us "the kingdom of heaven is at hand" (Matt. 4:17). He explains who will receive this kingdom (5:3). He tells his followers to pray for it, seek it, and proclaim it (6:10, 33; 10:7). He binds the satanic strong man and so demonstrates it (12:27–29). He promises to reveal its secrets (13:11). He describes it with parables (13:24, 31, 33, 44, 45, 47, etc.). And then . . .

He says that he will build his church, his *ekklēsia* (Matt. 16:18).

Wait a second—his what?

After so much talk about a kingdom, the word "church" might strike modern ears as a strange word to choose. A kingdom is a political thing. And a church is a religious thing, isn't it? Does Jesus change the subject? Apparently not, because right after saying he will build his church, he gives Peter, and by extension all the apostles, the "keys of the kingdom," apparently as the means by which this church will be built. So why then does he refer to an *ekklēsia*?

In fact, Jesus does choose a decidedly political and covenantal word, when he could use a word with a little less political resonance, like "synagogue."[5]

To understand this, let's do a five-century flashback from Jesus's day, like a television show that begins and then jumps to twenty-four hours earlier. I want to see if we can hear Jesus's term *ekklēsia* through first-century ears by backing up in the plotline. We start on the streets of fifth-century-BC Athens, where we hear playwrights like Euripides and historians like Thucydides using *ekklēsia* to refer to the gathering of full citizens of what they called the *polis*, or political community, for making decisions on judicial and political matters.[6] Any male citizen could attend an *ekklēsia*, debate, and vote by show of hands on officers and various proposals (votes in the courts occurred by ballot).[7] To do all that, of course, someone had to *be there*.

By the fourth century BC, Aristotle saw the powers of these *ekklēsiai* as relatively broad: "The assembly [*ekklēsia*] should be supreme over all causes, or at any rate over the most important."[8] Alexander the Great, who was tutored by Aristotle, brought the *polis* with its *ekklēsiai* to all the Greek cities of Asia and beyond. Alexander's successors eventually established thirty Greek cities in Palestine. By the time the New Testament was being written, the *ekklēsiai* had diminished in power and significance. The term could be used more broadly to refer to an unorganized crowd (as in Acts 19:32, 41). But organized assemblies continued to exist, as in Acts 19:38–39, where the town clerk of Ephesus tells a crowd to bring their charges to the courts or, if the courts don't satisfy their concerns, to settle them "in the regular assembly [*ekklēsia*]."[9]

What's interesting, furthermore, is that classical Greek treated the *ekklēsia* simply as the assembly. If you had said to Aristotle, "The *ekklēsia* is a people, not a place, right?" he would have looked at you cockeyed. "The people are the people," he would have said. "And to be an *ekklēsia* they have to gather in a place." In other words, classical Greek had one word for people (*dēmos*) and another word for assembly (*ekklēsia*). And so an *ekklēsia* was necessarily tied to the idea of a place. The people (*dēmos*) had to gather together in a place to become an assembly (*ekklēsia*).[10] Then, when the *ekklēsia* disbanded, the people would no longer be called an *ekklēsia* (see fig. 2).

Figure 2. *Ekklēsia* in classical Greek

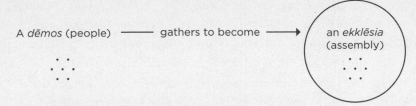

A *dēmos* (people) ——— gathers to become ———→ an *ekklēsia* (assembly)

We'll come back to this idea in the next chapter.

In the third century BC, a number of Jewish scholars began translating the Hebrew Bible into common Greek. The Greek translation, called the Septuagint, uses what would later be Jesus's term of choice, *ekklēsia*, to refer to the people of Israel gathered together, visibly demonstrating their nationhood under God.[11]

- The Israelites gathered at the base of Mount Sinai amid fire on "the day of the assembly"—the day of *ekklēsia* (Deut. 9:10; 10:4; 18:16).
- Rules of citizenship excluded certain people from worship in "the assembly of the LORD"—the *ekklēsia* of the Lord (Deut. 23:1–8).[12]
- Moses instructed "all Israel" to "assemble" every seven years to hear the words of the law, and then he offered his final charge to "the assembly of Israel"—the *ekklēsia* of Israel (Deut. 31:10–12, 30).
- Centuries later, King Solomon dedicated the temple by praying to God and then blessing "all the assembly of Israel" (2 Chron. 6:3).

The *ekklēsia* served a crucial role in making God's kingdom visible, as I said a moment ago.[13] God established his covenant with his people in the assembly.[14] And the people gathered to worship God in the assembly.

Sing to the LORD a new song,
his praise in the assembly [*ekklēsia*] of the godly! (Ps. 149:1)

Commentators today sometimes distinguish the political and religious usages of *ekklēsia*,[15] but the Hebrew mind would not have abided such a clean distinction. To bow before God as King is to bow before him as Redeemer. Indeed, God makes his rule visible precisely in order that he might be known and worshiped.

Further, the Greek Old Testament's use of *ekklēsia*, which translates the Hebrew *qahal*, is similar to classical Greek in that it refers only to the assembly.[16] Other words would be used to refer to the people who gather, especially *synagogue* (Hebrew: *edah*) and people (Hebrew: *am*). For example:

- "Then Moses and Aaron fell on their faces before all the assembly [Greek: *ekklēsia*; Hebrew: *qahal*] of the congregation [Greek: *synagōgē*; Hebrew: *edah*]" (Num. 14:5).
- "Assemble [Greek: *ekklēsiasas*; Hebrew: *qahal*] the people [Greek: *laos*; Hebrew: *am*]" (Deut. 31:12).

In other words, a first-century Jew who knew the Greek New Testament may have responded to the claim that "an *ekklēsia* is a people, not a place" the way I said Aristotle would have: "Well, yes, it's a people, but only because they are gathered in a place" (see fig. 3).

Figure 3. Terms used in Old Testament Greek and Hebrew

Gk.: A *synagōgē/laos*
Heb.: An *edah/am*
(congregation/people)

gathers
to become

Gk.: an *ekklēsia*
Heb.: a *qahal*
(assembly)

The *ekklēsia* or assembly of Israel was something that assembled. It visibly pictured a people worshiping and submitting themselves to the rule of God.

When God exiled Israel from the land, first the Northern Kingdom then the Southern, he effectively disbanded the assembly. Yet the prophet Joel, in the same breath in which he promised the out-pouring of God's Spirit (Joel 2:28–32; Acts 2:17–21), also told Israel to "gather the people" and "consecrate the congregation"—the *ekklēsia* (Joel 2:16). Israel's entire political career and national history is pictured as a gathering, then a scattering through exile, and then a promise of another gathering.

The New Testament's usage of *ekklēsia* does develop beyond what we see in classical and Old Testament usage, as we'll consider in the next chapter. For now, however, I want you to think about all this Greco-Roman and Jewish background[17] as you stop again and hear Jesus showing up and saying, "I will build my *ekklēsia*." Why did he pick that word?

Jesus had in mind a gathering of a new Israel.[18] Here was the true end of exile. Here was a new body politic. Here was the reconstituting of God's kingdom through outposts of that heavenly kingdom on earth. Jesus came to gather a new assembly, a new *ekklēsia*.[19]

No, Jesus did not intend his disciples to take over a geographic plot of land by sword. But nor did he intend for them to be a "religion" merely characterized by certain beliefs. Rather, he wanted to constitute them as a kingdom—a political reality. And so he chose a political word that necessarily came with spatial meaning: *ekklēsia*. His disciples would submit to him, and they would submit to him together. Visibly. In a place. As a testimony to his rule. As if they were a landed kingdom like any other kingdom.

Ancient Greco-Roman and Septuagint definitions of the word do not determine Jesus's definition. New Testament usage does. But it's not difficult to see how all this background would have struck those who heard Jesus. How differently first-century ears would have heard that word than we do. There were no marketplace intuitions for them, as in "I really enjoyed that church. That preacher was hilarious. But did you see good programs for the kids?"

Indeed, two chapters later, Jesus sounds more like Aristotle or like the courts that would have patrolled Israel's citizenship boundaries for purposes of worship (see Deut. 23:1–8):[20] "If he refuses to listen to them, tell it to the [*ekklēsia*/assembly] church. And if he refuses to listen even to the [*ekklēsias*/assembly] church, let him be to you as a Gentile and a tax collector" (Matt. 18:17). In this moment, Jesus treats the church as a judicial assembly acting together in judgment. The apostles followed suit. Decades later, Paul asks the Corinthian church, "Is it not those inside the church whom you are to judge?" (1 Cor. 5:12).

Church Authority: The Keys of the Kingdom and Agreement

Do you see how I'm trying to reshape our church intuitions? I'm connecting it to the language of kingdom and the political in order to infuse our vision of a local church with the concept of authority, as with the Greek legislative assembly or the Israelite people gathered to hear God's commands. The church is an authoritative body, like an embassy. The very word *ekklēsia* or "church" vibrates and glows with both kingdom and spatial significance. It is a political or authority-structured thing. And just as the idea of a kingdom typically invokes thoughts of a land or a place, so Jesus chooses a word for the people of this kingdom that necessarily invokes the idea of place—an assembly.

What's crucial to understand, next, is what role each individual member plays in making a church what it is, because that will help us further understand the necessity of a gathering. We'll discover that this authority is not just *over* us. It *is* us. We are all together the vibrating, glowing thing.

In Matthew 18, Jesus gives authority to these local *ekklēsiai*, these embassies of his kingdom. And in the process he defines the role that every member plays in the authority structure of a church. A church's authority, Jesus teaches, rests in our agreement with one another on the *what* and the *who* of the gospel. And this agreement can occur only by our gathering together.

Let me explain. The setting for the lesson is a hypothetical case of church discipline. Verse 15 presents the problem and the first round of evaluation and judgment: "If your brother sins against you, go and tell him his fault, between you and him alone. If he listens to you, you have gained your brother." "You" here is singular. So you as a church member must do your judicial duty of protecting the church, the *ekklēsia*, by rescuing a brother from his sin. Assuming you and the brother disagree, you must work for agreement by involving others.

Verse 16 then describes a second round of evaluation and judgment, this time invoking an old Jewish courtroom principle from Deuteronomy 19. Two or three must agree for a charge to stick: "But if he does not listen, take one or two others along with you, that every charge may be established by the evidence of two or three witnesses." Verse 17, which we just saw, locates the third round of evaluation and judgment in the assembly. The assembly is the final court of appeal. "If he refuses to listen to them, tell it to the church. And if he refuses to listen even to the church, let him be to you as a Gentile and a tax collector."

Verse 18 then offers the authoritative grounds by which the assembly can do this. The assembly possesses the keys of the kingdom for binding and loosing. "Truly, I say to you [plural], whatever you [pl.] bind on earth shall be bound in heaven, and whatever you [pl.] loose on earth shall be loosed in heaven." The keys are not explicitly mentioned here. But two chapters earlier Jesus gave Peter the keys to bind and to loose right after affirming both Peter and Peter's confession (see Matt. 16:15–20). Jesus had said to him, "I will give you [singular] the keys of the kingdom of heaven, and whatever you [sg.] bind on earth shall be bound in heaven, and whatever you loose [sg.] on earth shall be loosed in heaven" (16:19). The apostles held the keys to bind and loose, but so do churches.

To bind and loose is to do the work of a judge. A judge does not make law, and a judge does not make a person innocent or guilty. Rather, a judge interprets the law and then declares a judgment on a person with the pound of a gavel. He or she "binds" or "looses" someone by applying the law. Likewise, a church assembly, with keys of the kingdom in hand, does not *make* the gospel or *make* someone a Christian. Rather, the assembly is authorized here in Matthew 18 to say, "This is a right/wrong confession of the gospel" and "This is/is not a gospel confessor."

To summarize, the keys give a church the authority to render judgment on the *what* and the *who* of the gospel—to say, "This is our statement of faith" and "This person is a member." Or not.

That's what Jesus does when he affirms Peter and Peter's confession in Matthew 16. That's what the church does here in Matthew 18, only in reverse.

Verse 19 goes on to re-explain verses 15–18 ("Again I say to you"), and this is crucial, so make sure you follow. Jesus now takes the conversation beyond the church-discipline case study and applies it to any judicial matter that a church must decide upon, such as receiving members or affirming a statement of faith ("anything they ask"):[21] "Again I say to you, if two of you agree on earth about anything they ask, it will be done for them by my Father in heaven."

The word to focus on for the moment is "agree." If verse 18 locates church authority symbolically in the keys of the kingdom, verse 19 redescribes this authority as *an agreement*. The two or three witnesses in verse 16 must *agree* before taking a matter to the whole church. The members of the church in verse 17 must *agree* before excluding someone from membership as a final act of discipline. They must *agree* to bind or *agree* to loose. And behind all this, the members of a church must *agree* on who Jesus is, just like Jesus asked the disciples back in chapter 16. Is Jesus John the Baptist? Elijah? One of the prophets? Or the Christ, the Son of the living God? Only when they *agree* on who Jesus is can they *gather in his name*, as we'll consider from 18:20 in a moment.

The very heart of church authority is an *agreement* between believers. How does that make sense? Well, remember Jeremiah's new covenant promise granted every citizen equal political standing before God's throne (Jer. 31:34). No longer would there be a separate class of priests who could grant access to God. Instead, all would be priests, as Luther famously argued. As such, any church authority *over* a member of the new covenant—a Christian—must come *through the agreement of* the member. And to be sure, this authority is always *under* the word of God. But the church's authority exists when Christians *agree* upon what that word says. (As I said in the introduction, church order emerges organically from the gospel.)

To be a church, everyone, whether two or two thousand, must *agree* that they are talking about the same gospel (today we call this a statement of faith). And they must *agree* that the members of the church, as best they can tell, subscribe to the gospel (today we call this a membership directory). Working to ensure that we remain in agreement is one way to describe our priestly responsibility in the gospel (see 2 Cor. 6:14–7:1). In a case needing church discipline, of course, that agreement is breaking down.

This is why I said a moment ago that church authority is not just *over* us. It *is* us. We are the vibrating and glowing political thing. In other words, the authority I am describing here is the authority that actually *creates a local or particular* church. The authority of the keys, which is the authority of Christians agreeing with one another and shaking hands on it, is the authority that creates a church.

All that is very theological. So think instead of Oleg and Marina standing in the market and meeting Sergei for the first time. He mentioned words like "God," "blessings," and "prayer." They began to wonder, "Is he one of us?" They asked him. He answered. More questions about the gospel followed: Which Jesus do you believe in? Do you understand yourself to be a sinner saved by grace? Have you repented? What do you think the Bible is? Little by little both parties began to realize they *agreed* upon the gospel, as well as one another's membership in the gospel. And that *agreement* on earth formed the basis of an earthly covenant before the Father in heaven. They could *bind* each other by that agreement. And through that agreement and that mutual binding they became a church.

Hence, the 1644 London Baptist Confession, we saw a moment ago, defined a church as "a company of visible saints . . . joined to the Lord, and each other, by mutual agreement." Multisite pastor J. D.

Greear, likewise, rightly observes that a covenant—a mutually binding agreement—is of the essence of a church.[22]

Church authority, as we learn in Matthew 16 and 18, verse 19 especially, is two Christians shaking hands in agreement. They agree
on the gospel and their membership in the gospel.

The Gathering as the Temporary but
Visible Geography of the Kingdom

But there's one more step here. Just as people need to come together to shake hands, so the saints need to gather together in order
to formally share agreement as a church. So says Jesus by explicitly
identifying himself with *the gathering*. "For where two or three are
gathered in my name, *there* am I *among* them" (Matt. 18:20).

Like fifteenth-century Spanish explorers crossing oceans in
search of gold, here our ship runs aground on the temporary-but-
visible geography of Christ's kingdom: the gathering. It's temporary because it lasts on a weekly basis for only a couple of hours.
It's temporary because we have not yet attained our permanent
inheritance. But the geography is real nonetheless. It's spatial. It's
physical. It exists. It's not theoretical. It's visible. And it's where the
action happens.

Do you see them? Oleg, Marina, Sergei, Zena, Olga, Will, and his
wife? Squished together in an upstairs room together above the
kitchen? Several in chairs, others on the side of the bed, one or two
on the floor? The gospel actually produces its own kind of space.[23]

These are the two or three (or seven) gathered in Jesus's name,
meaning they *agree* on who he is, and they agree on one another's
professions of faith. They don't agree upon the Mormon Jesus or
the Jehovah's Witness Jesus or the Muslim Jesus. Rather, they can
say to one another: "You believe Jesus is God from God, Light from
Light, true God from true God, begotten, not made? Me too!"

Some want to argue that the two or three witnesses in Matthew
18:20 can be any small group in the church. Yet think about that
possibility. Every small group could then wield the authority of the

keys to create a church over and against the rest of the church. Each could receive members or excommunicate, or affirm its own statement of faith. But what would happen if one small group *agreed* on an act of excommunication and another didn't? Or a change in the statement of faith? Effectively, we would be witnessing a church split, because all these are the precise activities that make a church a church: groups of gathered people agreeing upon a gospel *what* and a gospel *who*. This gathered group who share agreement on these matters *is* the church. It's the basic unit of kingdom authority, whether that group consists of two or three or three thousand.

The ancient Jewish courtroom principle, where two or three witnesses make a charge stick, applies here in the gathering. They are bound together in a shared testimony or witness. The gathering and the agreement glue them together with a legal glue. It's not casual or spontaneous. It's formal and official.

Jesus then seals the gathering, he seals the agreement, he seals the activities of binding and loosing, with his own presence: "There am I among them."[24] What does it mean that he is among them? Does he hover as a mystical fog in the room? We know Jesus has physically ascended and is seated at the right hand of the Father in heaven. And we know the Spirit of Jesus indwells all those who belong to him, as John's Gospel tells us (John 14:17, 26; 15:26). Yet Matthew's Gospel does not speak about the Spirit in this fashion, and the incarnate Jesus refers to *his presence in the assembly*, not *the Spirit's presence in the believer*.

By saying he's present, quite simply, Jesus is identifying himself with this gathering and authorizing them as his assembly.[25] He is saying, "They're with me and I'm with them," the way Yahweh identified himself with the people of the Old Testament: "I am their God, and they are my people." Notice, too, that Jesus promises to "build" this people on a rock just like the temple was built upon a rock, the temple where God dwelled.

In contemporary parlance, we might say that the gathering is where Jesus's flag flies, the way a nation's flag flies at its embassies in foreign nations, identifying each embassy with its home nation. By extension, that means the actions of the gathering represent him, even though he has now ascended to heaven and possesses all authority in heaven and earth (Matt. 28:18). The gathering can bind and loose on earth, knowing that they speak for him and the Father in heaven, like ambassadors or embassies.

In this sense, Jesus is "there" (*ekei*). He is "among" (*en mesō*) them.[26] Jesus is *there* in the second-floor room at Sergei's house when the seven saints gather. He identifies with them and they represent him. Also, he is *there* at the 9:30 a.m. service and *there* at the 11:00 a.m. service of a multiservice church. He is *there* at the north campus and *there* at the south campus of a multisite church. He identifies with each assembly, and each assembly can therefore make binding and loosing decisions on behalf of heaven. Each assembly has all the binding and loosing authority that creates a church. Each has him. Each is a church.

Jesus does not say, "When saints gather at 9:00 and 11:00, I am *half there* and *half there*, *half among* the one group and *half among* the other, each of them half-way speaking for me." He says, "When the 9:00 a.m. gathers, I'm there. And when the 11:00 a.m. gathers, I am there. Both of them speak for me. Both represent my kingdom rule. You can see the geography of the kingdom in both places." And—I am contesting—he is saying, "Both are churches." So, too, with the north and south "campuses."

Furthermore, Jesus doesn't say, "I'm there with the unified budget, brand, and board of multiple campuses." The church-creating authority described in Matthew 18 does not rest in the leaders. It's not merely over us. It rests in us, the actual assembly. We're all *under* it and *in* it because it's our agreement with one another.

In a multisite or multiservice church, the leaders either possess key-wielding authority outright or at least are the mediators of the agreement. They are the unifying factor. You and I might attend different assemblies, yet somehow the leaders enact my agreement that you are a Christian, or your agreement that I should be

WHAT IF A SINGLE CHURCH SERVICE IS TOO BIG FOR PEOPLE TO KNOW ONE ANOTHER?

Multisite and multiservice advocates often claim that once a church reaches a certain size, church members cannot all know one another. So dividing up a church between services or sites, if anything, helps members in each site or service know one another better. Practically speaking, they might be right.

But what I'm arguing here is that a particular church on earth is *not* constituted simply by our relationships or fellowship. It's constituted by Christ's authority, which he gives to the gathering. Therefore, this particular argument misses the point of what constitutes the church. A regular gathering of twenty thousand people, gathered for preaching and the celebration of the ordinances, is *in principle* a church in a way that two services of ten persons apiece who all know one another is not a single church. Yes, the former will have significant pastoral challenges! It might even want to divide, much as God eventually scattered the church in Jerusalem. But it remains a church.

excommunicated. Inevitably, in other words, authority shifts upward onto their shoulders. Perhaps all this would be fine if Christianity were a faith of merely words and ideas. People make binding agreements all the time over the phone, through the Internet, through a messenger. But Jesus means for his kingdom not just to be audible but also to be visible and active. He means to keep words and lives together. The gathering is where that happens, even if there are ten thousand people and you cannot begin to know everyone. The principle remains the same: *This* is the assembly. *These* are God's citizens on earth. Do you see them? They formally affirm Christ's name and one another not just in word but also with their physical bodies.

If there is a proof text in the Bible for the one-assembly church, it's Matthew 18:20. A church requires more than what we find in this verse, like the ordinances, but not less. Indeed, we can narrow it down to three words: "gather," "there," "among." When two or three gather to affirm the gospel with the authority of heaven, Jesus is there among them, identifying his authority with theirs and saying they represent heaven.

The geography of Christ's kingdom shows up there temporarily but visibly.

How We Wield the Keys and Seal Our Agreement: Baptism and the Supper

How do believers gather in Jesus's name, formally shaking hands in agreement on the *what* and the *who* of the gospel? We do it through baptism and the Lord's Supper. Baptism is the doorway into a church, while the Lord's Supper is the regular family meal for the church.[27] As I've been saying, Matthew 18:20 doesn't give us everything we need to make a church. We also need the ordinances, which Jesus provides in Matthew 26 and 28. These enact our agreement with one another.

First, Jesus establishes the Supper in Matthew 26. He gives it as a sign of inclusion in the new covenant. Paul then connects the Supper with the church: "Because there is one bread," he says, "we who are many are one body, for we all partake of the one bread" (1 Cor. 10:17; cf. 11:29). Therefore, he tells us to "wait for one another" when we "come together as a church" for the Supper (1 Cor. 11:18, 33). Partaking of the bread shows that we are one body. It reveals who the body of Christ is. It makes us visible to the world and each other. The Supper, we might say, makes the invisible church visible.

Second, Jesus establishes baptism in Matthew 28. Yet several textual clues tell us to read Matthew 28 in light of Matthew 16 and 18. Presumably, the ones who bind and loose in heaven and earth (Matt. 18) are subject to the one with all authority in heaven and earth (Matt. 28). Presumably, the ones who gather in his name

(Matt. 18) are the ones to baptize in his name (Matt. 28). And, presumably, the ones with whom he dwells now (Matt. 18) are the ones with whom he will dwell always (Matt. 28).

The difference between the universal church and the local church, we might say, is that the local involves both geography and the exercise of church authority, which is exercised through the ordinances.

Picture it this way: two individuals are shipwrecked on an island with a Bible. They each read it and come to faith. Their first act of "agreement" in that faith would be shown in baptizing each other (cf. Acts 8:26–39). And through that baptism they would have taken the first step in becoming a church.[28] For them to be a church on an ongoing basis would require them to affirm one another by sharing the Supper.

Or think of missionary Will asking the Ural Mountain group if they were ready to commit themselves to one another—to commit to being a church. Oleg recognized that all they lacked was the Lord's Supper. Participating in the Supper that day, and then on an ongoing basis, made them a visible, particular church. The ordinances "put a visible difference between those that belong unto the church, and the rest of the world," says the Westminster Confession (27.1).

What Is a Church?

We have covered a lot of territory in this chapter. First, we have sought to re-form our church intuitions by considering the crucial role of authority based on the Bible's kingdom storyline.

Second, we have discovered that the word "church" or *ekklēsia* is a political one, which speaks to the very nature of what a church is and what the gathering is.

Third, we have seen that Jesus gives the whole congregation authority to create itself as a local church through agreeing upon who he is and agreeing with one another's membership in him—the *what* and the *who* of the gospel.

Fourth, we have seen that Jesus ties his presence to any of these gatherings where people agree with one another in this binding fashion.

And fifth, we have learned that we conduct all this business through the ordinances.

Can we delocalize the early Protestant definitions of a local church? No, we can't, and for three reasons. First, a gathering is necessary for people to shake hands or mutually agree with one another, at least in the word-and-body fashion envisioned by Jesus and Old Testament courtroom rules.

Second, perhaps most importantly, Jesus explicitly identifies with the gathering.

Third, the gathering makes God's kingdom actually and concretely visible.

Remarkably, this is what we see in the church in Jerusalem in the opening chapters of Acts. "And they were all together in Solomon's Portico," this five-football-field-long structure on the east side of the temple.[29] The kingdom of God became visible among them—*there*. "None of the rest dared join them," Luke continues, "but the people held them in high esteem. And more than ever believers were added to the Lord, multitudes of both men and women" (Acts 5:12–14). There they baptized and—presumably—partook of the Lord's Supper. In these early and unusual days, in fact, the church met every day in the temple and in their homes, perhaps like small groups in our day. They shared food, possessions, financial resources, even homes and properties with one another (Acts 2:42–47; 4:32–37).

So it was in Corinth. Paul even seems to borrow from Jesus's instruction (Matt. 18:20) to address a matter of excommunication in Corinth: "When you are assembled in the name of the Lord Jesus and my spirit is present, with the power of our Lord Jesus . . ." (1 Cor. 5:4). We just heard Paul's call for the people to wait for one another in receiving the Supper. And he offers very clear guidelines for their worship assemblies together in chapter 14. We'll return to

Jerusalem, Corinth, and a few other New Testament churches in chapter 2.

For now, think back to Oleg and Marina praying for a church. They had already heard the gospel and had repented and believed. Yet they knew something was missing. With the gospel in their hearts, they suddenly felt like aliens or exiles in foreign territory, even if they were Russian citizens living in Russia. Something in them desired their new homeland. And so they prayed for a church, where they would find the fellowship, oversight, and instruction of other saints. They wanted safe harbor. So they came together and became *a* church. Yet, since every church, no matter how small, represents the whole church, they became not just *a* church but *the* church.[30]

What is a church? It's an embassy of Christ's kingdom. It's a group of Christians who together identify themselves and each other as followers of Jesus and as *the* church through regularly gathering (in one place at one time) in his name, preaching the gospel, and celebrating the ordinances. All this they do by the authority of the keys.

So next time you hear someone say, "The church is a people, not a place," you might respond: "Sort of. The people become a people by regularly assembling in a place. You can't call the team a team if they never play together."

THE WORK OF THE GATHERED CHURCH

What does the gathering do? The following:*

Glorifies God. All of life should be spent this way (1 Cor. 10:31), yet the gathering declares this purpose (see Eph. 3:10, 21).

Exemplifies the church. We are God's people, Christ's body, the Spirit's temple, the shepherd's flock, the vine's branch, the kingdom's citizens, the demonstration of God's wisdom and grace. And the assembly illustrates all of this. Insiders and outsiders alike can *see* this, *experience* this, *feel* these things in the assembly (1 Cor. 11:17–34; 13; 14:1, 3–5, 12, 33).

Edifies the saints. Everything done in the gathering should be for building up the saints, Paul teaches (see 1 Cor. 14:4, 12, 26; Eph. 5:19; Col. 3:16).

Expresses and promotes fellowship. The assembly *expresses* fellowship. We enjoy it then and there. And the assembly *promotes* fellowship. It encourages us to fellowship together on Monday to Saturday (see Heb. 10:23–25).

Impresses outsiders. Christians will evangelize throughout the week, yes, but the assembly itself possesses evangelistic power. The seeker-sensitive or attractional church gets this much right (see 1 Cor. 14:24–25).

Commemorates and proclaims salvation. The assembly commemorates and proclaims salvation. Paul states very clearly that "as often as you eat this bread and drink the cup, you proclaim the Lord's death until he comes" (1 Cor. 11:26).

Illumines and affirms the members of the people of God. Baptism names us with Christ (Matt. 28:19), and the Supper reveals who the body of Christ is (1 Cor. 10:17; see also 11:29). The reverse of this occurs in the discussion of church discipline in 1 Corinthians 5, where Paul tells the church that the unrepentant sinner should "be removed" from their fellowship (v. 2).

* The first six points come from Everett Ferguson, *The Churches of Christ: A Biblical Ecclesiology for Today* (Grand Rapids, MI: Eerdmans, 1996), 244–46. I added the seventh.

2

A CHURCH IS AN ASSEMBLY

If you own one, pull your favorite Greek-English lexicon off the shelf, and turn to the entry for ἐκκλησία, or *ekklēsia*, or "church."

As a seminary graduation gift, my then-fiancée, now wife, gave me the third edition of Bauer, Danker, Arndt, and Gingrich's *A Greek-English Lexicon of the New Testament and Other Early Christian Literature*, or BDAG for short. It's a large and beautiful volume, with Smyth-sewn binding that sits comfortably open on a desk. I was very grateful for her gift, since the $175 list price was well beyond my seminary means.

BDAG was and remains the gold standard for biblical Greek-to-English lexicons, sort of like the Merriam Webster Dictionary for American English or the Oxford English Dictionary for British English. My fellow seminary students always spoke about BDAG with reverence, as if white velvet gloves might be the best way to handle it. The volume had begun its life in German in the early twentieth century and gone through several editions before being translated into English in 1957. A second English edition came out in 1979, followed by the third in 2000. I began seminary in January 2001, and older students "in the know" were still absorbing the shock of the fact that the Lutheran lexicographer F. W. Danker had moved his "D" from the last position in the second edition (BAGD) to the second position in the third edition (BDAG). He was lead editor on the third, and B, A, and G were all dead. The apparent land grab raised a few seminarian eyebrows.

Ah, the things that seminarians get excited about!

I am sure I had read BDAG's definition of *ekklēsia* before, but it was with some dismay several months ago that I discovered afresh that BDAG's definition contradicts the main point of this book. On pages 303–4, you will find the following in expanded fashion. I have put the relevant bits in boldface:

1. a regularly summoned legislative body, *assembly*, Ac 19:39.
2. a casual gathering of people, *an assemblage, gathering*, Ac 19:32, 40.
3. people with shared belief, *community, congregation*
   a. of OT Israelites *assembly, congregation*, Dt 31:30; Judg 20:2; Ac 7:38.
   b. of Christians in a specific place or area.
      α. of a specific Christian group *assembly, gathering* ordinarily involving worship and discussion of matters of concern to the community: Mt 18:17; 1 Cor 11:18; 14:12, 28, 35; Ro 16:5; Col 4:15; Phlm 2.
      β. *congregation* or *church* as **the totality of Christians living and meeting in a particular locality or larger geographical area, but not necessarily limited to one meeting place**: Ac 5:11; 8:3; 9:31; 11:26; 12:5; 15:3; 18:22; 20:17; 1 Cor 4:17; Phil 4:15; 1 Ti 5:16; Js 5:14; 3 J 9f. **More definitely of the Christians in Jerusalem** Ac 8:1; 11:22; 15:4, 22; Cenchreae Ro 16:1; Corinth 1 Cor 1:2; 2 Cor 1:1; Laodicea Col 4:16; Rv 3:14; Thessalonica 1 Th 1:1; 2 Th 1:1; Colossae Phlm l.
   c. the global community of Christians, *(universal) church*: Mt 16:18; Ac 9:31; 1 Cor 6:4; 12:28; Eph 1:22; 3:10, 21; 5:23ff, 27, 29, 32; Col 1:18, 24; Phil 3:6:
      α. [church of God] 1 Cor 1:2; 10:32; 11:16; Gal 1:13; 1 Th 2:14; Ac 20:28.

β. [church of Christ] Ro 16:16.
γ. [church of God the Father and the Lord Jesus Christ] 1 Th 1:1.
δ. [the first, spiritual church] 2 Cl[ement] 14:1.

Most of this definition is unproblematic. It's the boldfaced portion of bβ that I find most troubling: "*congregation* or *church* as the totality of Christians living and meeting in a particular locality or larger geographical area, but not necessarily limited to one meeting place." That one sub-point is different from the others. Every other sub-point envisions an actual assembly; even the universal church does, which is a heavenly and eschatological gathering that meets even now (Eph. 2:7; Heb. 12:23). But Danker, together with Bauer, Arndt, and Gingrich, read verses cited in section bβ —and I included all of them[1]—and concluded that the word "church" does not necessarily describe something which actually assembles.

So open your Bible to the introduction of 1 Corinthians 1. You'll see that Paul greets "the church of God that is in Corinth" (1 Cor. 1:2). Since you see that the word "church" is singular, you might think it refers to the assembling of the saints in Corinth. But if you knew your Bible better (the lexicographers reason), as well as a little history on the small size of homes in Corinth, or something like that, then you would know that the "church" in Corinth actually consisted of multiple congregations or house churches. Any given occurrence of the word might refer to the whole city church, or it might refer to one of the city church's congregations. Call them campuses or sites, if you want.

Now, the editors of BDAG know that determining the definition of a word is always a matter of judgment based on usage, and some judgments are clearer than others. They want us to know, for instance, that the distinction between "church" and "congregation" is "more definitely" right for "the Christians in Jerusalem." Did you see that note in the definitions above? "Maybe we're wrong about the others," the editors seem to be saying, "but we are *more definitely* not wrong here." Acts 5:11 may refer to "the whole church," and 8:1 to "the church in Jerusalem," but several other texts refer to the Jerusalem church meeting in "their homes" and "from house to house" (see Acts 2:46; 5:42; 8:3). The inference follows: the church in Jerusalem definitely consisted of multiple house churches, congregations, campuses. Or, at least, it "more definitely" did (which is not quite "most definitely").

Could BDAG be right? Does Luke or Paul or do the other New Testament authors use the word *ekklēsia* in the singular to refer to something that never or seldom assembles? If they do, then the multisite model would seem to be legitimate.

Making an argument against the multisite model requires more than responding to a few pragmatic pastors. It means taking on a decent-sized swath of Greek scholarship.

A Lexicon Journey

I admit, the BDAG entry made me wonder. Was I wrong? One-assembly advocates routinely affirm, *"Ekklēsia* means assembly." But maybe it's not that simple. Another famous Greek dictionary observes that the New Testament moves back and forth between the singular and plural forms of *ekklēsia* "promiscuously."[2]

Talk about something that will raise seminarian eyebrows. The Bible's use of *ekklēsia* is *promiscuous*.

Curiosity took hold of me. Was line bβ in BDAG a recent development in the history of Greek-English lexicons? Maybe this lexical distinction between the whole city "church" and the smaller "congregations" was unique to recent scholarship.

I emailed a friend who had the 1979 second edition. He photographed the pages and texted them over. They showed the local-church usages of *ekklēsia* divided into three subheadings: "a church meeting" (citing 1 Cor. 11:18 etc.); "the church or congregation as the totality of Christians living in one place" (citing Matt. 18:17; Acts 5:11; 8:3; 1 Cor. 4:7; etc.); and "house churches" (citing

Rom. 6:5 etc.).[3] That's slightly less clear than the third edition, but seems to be tending in that direction.

What about the 1957 first edition, then? I found the volume at a nearby university library. It said exactly the same thing as the second.[4]

Maybe if I took the investigation even further back in time, I would find proof for my hypothesis.

A brief journey into older lexicons followed. I managed to find ten ranging from the late eighteenth to the early twentieth centuries that offered substantive definitions—something with more than a one- or two-word definition like "a church." To summarize what's pertinent, six of them said the word *ekklēsia* referred either to the universal church or to the gathered local church,[5] which made my case. One referred to a "local portion of the church," as well as a "congregation."[6] I honestly don't know what that means. Yet three of them divided the local church into both a larger "church" and smaller "congregations," including the oldest lexicon I found.[7] The second edition of *A Greek and English Lexicon to the New Testament*, written by John Parkhurst and published in 1794,[8] refers in one subheading to "a particular or single congregation of Christians" and in another subheading to "a particular church, though consisting of several congregations."[9] To put the point plainly, this eighteenth-century scholar argued that the Bible uses the word "church" in a way that's perfectly consistent with a multisite structure.

My hypothesis was mistaken. The distinction between "church" and "congregation" isn't recent among the lexicographers, those titans of Greek scholarship. It goes back at least to 1794.

High Church Instincts

Shortly after this investigation, I sat down to read the lengthy study of the term *ekklēsia* in Gerhard Kittel's formidable *Theological Dictionary of the New Testament*. If my fellow seminarians revered BDAG, they feared "Kittel," as it's known. It's a ten-volume beast, filled with liberal German scholarship and exhaustive word studies. My dad had bought me a water-damaged set for $100 from a pastor friend of his. The author of the entry on *ekklēsia* doesn't quite answer the question about whether a single city "church" might be composed of multiple congregations. He does argue we should always translate *ekklēsia* as "assembly" since every "individual congregation represents the whole body" and is "just as visible and corporeal as the individual man."[10] A good theological point.

Also, quite intriguingly, he observes that lexicographers tend to view the relationship between the universal and local church—between the one church and the many congregations—in a manner that suits their denominational affiliations.[11]

That sparked another question: how might the six authors compare to the three authors in terms of their denominational affiliations? I doubled back on the journey and, interestingly, discovered that all three scholars who lexically distinguished between one church and its multiple congregations were Anglicans. Meanwhile, the six authors who referred only to the universal and the local church consisted of a Congregationalist minister, the Presbyterian son of a Congregationalist minister, a Baptist, a Unitarian, an Anglican, and an unknown.

The sample of nine hardly meets the statistical standard of a couple thousand for a scientifically legitimate survey. But intuitions do matter. Could it be that someone who belongs to the Church of England—comprising many congregations—is more likely to assume the "Church of Corinth" or the "Church of Jerusalem" looked the same? The same principle would apply to the four names associated with BDAG, three of whom were Lutherans and therefore members of a larger denominational entity called a "church."

High church instincts, which locate the essence of the church closer to the bishops or to synodical structures, presumably influence how one regards the *"ekklēsia"* in the biblical text.

That said, high church intuitions may ironically parallel low church mega-multisite-church ones. These latter instincts will have been formed not by a centuries-old ecclesial hierarchy but by a market-proven charismatic leader, one who can unite multiple congregations. Multisite definitions, as we have seen, emphasize "a common vision, budget, leadership, and board."[12] They say nothing about *the people* uniting a multisite church. Megachurch leaders don't typically do the careful biblical work of a high church lexicographer, but they share this instinct: the essence of a church, or the thing that unites a church, dwells above the congregation. In both cases, it's almost apostolic. The high churchers draw a line of descent from the apostles through the bishops. The low church megachurchers envision a kind of apostolic charisma. Hence, the defenders of the mega-multisite churches often speak in terms of stewarding a man's unique gifts.

Pushing Mainstream

In fact, the mega-multisite-church phenomenon suggests that my original historical hypothesis might have been onto something. Once upon a time, it was the high churchers who were more likely to envision a church made up of multiple congregations. These days, however, a variety of factors have pushed that idea mainstream among the high churcher and the low.[13]

For instance, the ordained Baptist minister Eugene Nida and his coauthor Johannes Louw assert in their more recent *Greek-English Lexicon of the New Testament* that, in some contexts, *ekklēsia* can be translated as "group of those who trust in Christ." They continue, "Sometimes, as in 1 Cor 1:2, it is possible to translate 'Paul writes to the believers in Christ who live in Corinth.'"[14] The idea of an assembly is almost entirely evacuated from the Corinthian *ekklēsia*.

What's pushed the mainstream in this direction? Denominational identity and polity convictions play a much smaller role these days than in previous centuries, as Nida himself demonstrates, having grown more ecumenical in later life.[15] Christians are less convinced than ever that the Bible addresses church order.[16] Market-driven church-growth principles increasingly govern our approach to church, as mentioned a couple of chapters ago. God's good gift of creativity is treated as a crucial value for thinking through church structure.[17] More recently, video technology enables us to conceive of church structures that we never would have conceived of before.

Scholars also point to increased historical understanding of first-century houses. Biblical archeologists offer remarkable accounts of first-century homes and meeting spaces, down to the exact measurements.[18] Based on the size of those houses, as well as estimates concerning how many people attended churches, the experts conclude that all the Christians in a city surely could not have been in one place. New Testament commentator Richard Hays does just this with the church in Corinth:

> Such houses could have accommodated no more than thirty to fifty people for the common meal. It is, therefore, likely that there were several separate house church gatherings, meeting in the homes of leaders such as Stephanus ([1 Cor.] 16:15–18).... If each of the factions mentioned in 1:12 represents a different house church (a possible but uncertain assumption), there might have been as many as 150 to 200 Christians in the city at the time of Paul's writing.[19]

George Eldon Ladd says the same thing: "It is difficult to believe that such a meeting place would be large enough to accommodate all the Christians in a given city."[20]

Yet, as Hays concedes, these kinds of historical reconstructions depend finally on speculation. In some instances, I would add, they flatly contradict Scripture, as we will consider in a moment regarding Corinth. Furthermore, recent scholarship suggests that the houses of the wealthy could have accommodated quite a bit more than the commonly assumed fifty.[21] And there is no reason to assume churches met only in houses.[22]

Still, the assumption sticks: large gatherings were impossible. I recall one conversation with a multisite pastor over lunch. I was trying to avoid sharing my opinion on multisite churches, but he knew I was writing this book, so he kept pushing. He was making Hays and Ladd's point: "We know that no buildings in these cities could have accommodated all the members of the church."

After so much pushing, I finally had to say something. I opened the Bible app on my phone and read, "And the twelve summoned the full number of the disciples" (Acts 6:2). "That included over five thousand men, right?" I said.

He replied, "Sure, sure, but we *know* they could not have fit in one place."

I looked at him, blinked a couple of times, then looked down at my Bible app and read again, "And the twelve summoned the full number of the disciples." I looked up a second time without saying more.

He meagerly offered, "Right, okay. I guess that makes sense."

Our assumptions and intuitions are so strong, we can have a hard time seeing *what the Holy Spirit–inspired text actually says*.

Assumption + Assumption = Certainty?

Sometimes historical background knowledge is crucial for interpreting Scripture. But the biblical justifications for multisite churches is rife with phrases like "Well, surely the early church must have . . ." or "We can assume they did not . . ."

For instance, Roger Gehring's *House Church and Mission* offers the most exhaustive biblical argument I'm aware of for a citywide "church" plus individual "congregations," or what I will call multisite for simplicity's sake. Gehring's book is a favorite go-to scholarly study for supporting the multisite position. His argument is this:

> The early Christian movement was characterized by the coexistence of two church forms: the house church and the whole church at any given locale. This means that, in the various cities, alongside the local church as a whole there existed house churches in which most of the activities and life of the church took place.[23]

75

Gehring's book is packed with textual and in-depth background research. Yet I would encourage anyone to read through his textual case city by city and start looking for words like "assume" or "if" or "probably." I've italicized a few:

- "Therefore we can *assume* a plurality of house churches for Philippi" (132).
- "It can also be *assumed* that more than one group existed in Thessalonica, and this would indicate a plurality of house churches here as well" (133).
- "*If our conclusions are correct*, then in Corinth there existed a plurality of house churches" (142).
- "The text does not explicitly mention a house [in Cenchreae], but verse 2 *implies* one" (142).
- "This . . . *suggests* a plurality of house churches [in Ephesus], but we cannot be certain" (144).
- "The house church of Nympha is *probably* in Laodicea. . . . *If* Nympha's house church can be located in Laodicea, we *would have* a house church within the overall local church in that area" (155).
- "It *appears that traces* of two additional house churches can also be observed in Rom 16:14, 15" (157).
- "It is *almost certain* that a plurality of house churches existed in Rome" (Rom 16)" (296).

I'm grateful that orthodox books on the doctrine of the Trinity or the resurrection or justification don't read like this. Yet, add all Gehring's *maybes* together and what do we get? Somehow, we get a *certainty*: "A plurality of house churches was *demonstrated with certainty* for Rome, probably for Thessalonica, and possibly for Ephesus, Philippi, and Laodicea, and the coexistence of a number of house churches alongside the local church as a whole *was demonstrated* for Corinth" (159).

I confess, the math eludes me. Assumption + assumption + assumption = "certainty" and "demonstrated"? In fact, none of

Gehring's claims is demonstrated. They're all supposed. The biblical text does not demonstrate any of this, which tells me that intuitions and desires drive the exegesis.

To be sure, we are all susceptible to this risk. My biases guide me as well. I don't deny it. Which is precisely why, when we turn to Scripture itself, we must work to set aside, for at least a moment, what *must have been the case* based on our ingenious historical reconstructions and focus instead on what *is the case* in inspired Scripture. That is one step that will help us *not* read our intuitions into the Bible.

Let me propose this: We journeyed through a few lexicons. Let's take two more trips. First, let's take a word-search journey on *ekklēsia* through the New Testament. Then let's travel through some of the major biblical cities and look at what the Bible actually says about what's in those cities: one site or several?

Word Search on *Ekklēsia*

Open your favorite Bible website, your Bible software, or your concordance, and skim over all the New Testament usages of *ekklēsia*. Or, better, turn to appendix 1 in this book, where I list and categorize all of them. Here's the question I have been asking while staring at every usage: Is there a sense in which the word *ekklēsia* is ever used without a view to an assembly?

Here's why I'm asking it that way. As I've said, Christians often remark, "The church is not a place; it's a people." And there are biblical reasons to speak this way. Luke says about the church in Antioch, "And when they arrived and gathered [*sunagagontes*] the church [*ekklēsian*] together, they declared all that God had done with them" (Acts 14:27). Notice the subtle distinction in Luke's usage between "the church" and the act of gathering. The church, apparently, preexists that particular gathering, such that the assembly (church) could then assemble. The church in Acts 14:27 is the people who assemble, not the assembly per se.

Further, this is not an isolated incident. Keep one finger on this page, and turn to the appendix on uses of *ekklēsia*. You'll see I placed them in five categories based on my own sense of usage. I used the ESV translation, but I substituted the word *ekklēsia*/"assembly" or *ekklēsiai*/"assemblies" (regardless of case endings) for the word "church" or "churches."

Category 1 includes every instance where, by my judgment, the word "assembly" appears to be used with a view to the assembly or gathering. Therefore, I inserted the *interpretive* phrase in brackets "gathering of members" in order to suggest one could read the word *ekklēsia* or assembly as "gathering of members." For instance:

- *Matthew 18:17.* "If he refuses to listen to them, tell it to the *ekklēsia*/assembly [gathering of members]. And if he refuses to listen even to the *ekklēsia*/assembly [gathering of members] let him be to you as a Gentile and a tax collector."
- *Acts 11:22.* "The report of this came to the ears of the *ekklēsia*/assembly [gathering of members] in Jerusalem, and they sent Barnabas to Antioch."
- *Romans 16:5.* "Greet also the *ekklēsia*/assembly [gathering of members] in their house."

You might disagree with any one of my judgments for what belongs in this category, but hopefully you can still affirm the legitimacy of the category.

Category 2 presents every instance where the word "assembly" appears to be used *without* a view to the act of assembling or gathering. The focus is on the people—their identity as a marked-off group. For instance, when someone who is sick calls for "the elders of the *ekklēsia*/assembly" (James 5:14), I assume the sick person is not calling them from the assembly itself. He's calling the leaders of the membership. Therefore, I have inserted the interpretative words "members" or "membership" into brackets, suggesting that you could read *ekklēsia* synonymously with its members. For instance:

- *Acts 8:1, 3.* "And Saul approved of his execution. And there arose on that day a great persecution against the *ekklēsia*/

assembly [members/membership] in Jerusalem, and they were all scattered throughout the regions of Judea and Samaria, except the apostles. . . . But Saul was ravaging the *ekklēsia*/assembly [members/membership], and entering house after house, he dragged off men and women and committed them to prison."

- *Romans 16:1*. "I commend to you our sister Phoebe, a servant of the *ekklēsia*/assembly [members/membership] at Cenchreae."
- *1 Corinthians 5:12*. "For what have I to do with judging outsiders? Is it not those inside the *ekklēsia*/assembly [membership] whom you are to judge?"

As with category 1, you might disagree with any number of my judgments, but hopefully you'll grant the legitimacy of the category.

Category 3 lists those occurrences where the word *ekklēsia* could be read either way. Or rather, it's just not clear to me whether we should list these particular verses with category 1 or 2.

Category 4 points to the universal church, which I understand to be a heavenly and/or eschatological assembly. This is most explicit in the Hebrews 12 text. Yet it's a property of an already–not yet eschatology in all these texts.

Category 5 points to general civic usage. So the verses in categories 2 and 3 are what provoke the question of whether the word *ekklēsia* or "assembly" can be used apart from an assembly or a gathering. They also seem to give rise to BDAG's category *"congregation* or *church* as the totality of Christians living and meeting in a particular locality or larger geographical area, but not necessarily limited to one meeting place." In other words, if there is anything in the New Testament that undermines my argument that the Greek word *ekklēsia* always has an assembly in mind, it could very well be these verses in categories 2 and 3.

Remember, neither classical Greek nor the Greek Old Testament used the word *ekklēsia* this way. Classical Greek, for instance, distinguished between *dēmos* and *ekklēsia*, with the latter referring to an actual assembly. When the Athenian *ekklēsia* disbanded and everyone went home, they remained *the people* of Athens, but they were no longer the *ekklēsia*.[24] In classical Greek, we observed the dynamic shown in figure 4.

Figure 4. *Ekklēsia* in classical Greek

We see this same kind of usage in the New Testament, as when the town clerk calms the Ephesians rioters by saying, "But if you seek anything further, it shall be settled in the regular assembly [*ekklēsia*]" (Acts 19:39). The narrator continues: "And when he had said these things, he dismissed the assembly [*ekklēsian*]" (v. 41). In neither instance does the word specify a group of people that exists *as a group* before or after the assembly.

Yet, with categories 2 and 3 above, Jesus and the apostles expand how the word is used. It's as if *ekklēsia* keeps its own spot but also replaces *dēmos*. The *ekklēsia* is a people *and* a gathering. The people remain an *ekklēsia* whether or not they are actually assembled. Where Athenians might have said, "The people assemble," it's as if the biblical authors are willing to say, "The assembly assembles."

How does this make sense?

There are two ways we might make sense of what's going on. First, multisiters seem willing to say that *ekklēsia* can refer to something that never actually assembles. So the members of separate sites assemble. But the whole thing called a "church" (all the sites or services) doesn't actually assemble. It's as if the *ekklēsia* (assembly) becomes the *dēmos* (people) and is no longer an *ekklēsia* (assembly) at all, at least for some occurrences of the word (see fig. 5).

Figure 5. *Ekklēsia* according to the multisite model

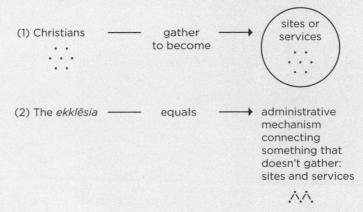

That really would be quite an evolved usage from the classical Greek! It's an assembly that never assembles. Parts of the church gather, but the church *itself* doesn't actually gather, at least by definitional necessity. It leaves one wondering why Jesus picked the word that had always meant "assembly" both in classical Greek and in the Septuiagint. Why didn't he just pick a word that meant "people," like *dēmos* or something else?

However, there is a more natural way to understand category 2, and that's to understand the New Testament's usage of the word *ekklēsia* like we understand the English word "team," as I mentioned earlier in the book. To be a member of a soccer team, you have to come together to play soccer. Gathering to play is an essential element of being a team and of belonging to the team. Yet "team" is also an identity-marker word. It refers to a group of people who remain in that group even when they are not doing the thing that makes them a group. So we can say, "The team spent the evening in the hotel." If the New Testament word *ekklēsia* works like the English word "team," then a church becomes a church by regularly assembling, but they remain a church even if they are not gathered at every moment (see fig. 6).

Figure 6. *Ekklēsia* in the New Testament
(like the English word "team")

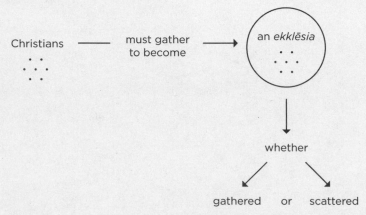

By this explanation, any given use of the word might lean more in one direction or another—with more of a view to the people assembled or with more of a view to *the people* who assemble. Yet never can the word *ekklēsia* finally be separated from the idea of *assembly*.

Which would explain how we could have both category 1 and category 2. Category 1 would refer to *the members assembled*, while category 2 would refer to *the members constituted by assembling* or *characterized by reoccurring assemblies.*[25]

If the second explanation for category 2 is correct, it's not quite right to say, "The church is a people, not a place." It might therefore be slightly better to say, "The church is a people who regularly gather in one place" or "a people whose place is the gathering."

So which explanation for category 2 is correct? Since classical Greek and Septuagintal usages keep the words tied pretty tightly to category 1, it seems to me that the burden of proof is on multisiters to demonstrate that the New Testament does actually use *ekklēsia* in a way that's entirely divorced from the assembly—all *dēmos* and no *ekklēsia*, by the standards of classical usage. For instance, if they could point to gatherings of Christians that do what churches do (preaching, ordinances, etc.) and that don't gather with other similar groups, and yet all those groups together are called "a church," they would prove their point. Can they?

That brings us to our second biblical journey—this one through a number of New Testament cities. The goal here is to discern whether the Bible envisions a citywide church made up of multiple congregations that belong to that one church—a multisite church.

Starting in Corinth

Corinth is a favorite for multisiters. We start there. Gehring and others spy out several house churches based on the following statements:[26]

1. "[Paul] went to see them, and because he was of the same trade he stayed with them and worked, for they were tentmakers by trade" (Acts 18:2–3).
2. "And [Paul] left there and went to the house of a man named Titius Justus, a worshiper of God. His house was next door to the synagogue" (Acts 18:7).
3. "Crispus, the ruler of the synagogue, believed in the Lord, together with his entire household. And many of the Corinthians hearing Paul believed and were baptized" (Acts 18:8).
4. "I did baptize also the household of Stephanas" (1 Cor. 1:16; see also 16:15–17).
5. "Erastus, the city treasurer, and our brother Quartus, greet you" (Rom. 16:23).

Here are the five purported house churches that make up "the church of God that is in Corinth" (1 Cor. 1:2). I have shown you the evidence—all of it.

Now, ask yourself, standing street-side looking through the front windows of these five houses, what do you see? Do you see a church service? I confess that I don't, even when I squint.

Gehring offers a rationale for each.

- Looking through house window 1, Gehring observes that Prisca and Aquila hosted house churches in Rome and Ephesus. So he supposes they *probably* hosted one here as well (Rom. 16:5; 1 Cor. 16:9).
- Window 2: Titius Justus was obviously influential and had big houses. So it could have been a house church.
- Window 3: The same for Crispus.
- Window 4: Stephanus's whole household was baptized, so he must have hosted a house church.
- Window 5: Archeologists found an old Corinthian inscription that documents a magistrate named Erastus, which means Erastus was probably wealthy, which means he had a big home, which means "everything appears to support the view that Erastus . . . served as a host to a house church in Corinth."[27]

That's the argument—all of it. Basically, the argument is, "They *could* have, so they *must* have."

Meanwhile, say Gehring and others, we can surmise that all these house churches gathered together as a city church because Paul refers to the "whole church" coming together (1 Cor. 14:23; also Rom. 16:23). It would be redundant to refer to the "whole" church if "church" already means an assembly of all the members. So Paul *must be* referring to all of the house churches coming together. Together the separate house churches add up to "the whole church."[28]

That is the biblical evidence—all of it—which compels the Gehrings and Hayses and Ladds and others to say, each in his own way, "Corinth is multisite."

Again, what do you think? "Erastus, the city treasurer, greets you." If you were on a jury, would these words compel you to conclude, "House church—right there"?

I have slowed us down on the sidewalks of Corinth because commentators throw out Bible references like these, offer a "well probably," and then breezily move us along, as if everyone just saw what they themselves saw. We could return to all five examples and offer counterarguments. The fact that Prisca and Aquila house a church in one city doesn't mean they do in every other city. That people are wealthy doesn't mean they host a house church. A household is not the same thing as a house church. And so forth. But never mind any alternative constructions. Just go back and look at the five verses. What do you *see*? Do you *see* a church or the constituting activities of a church?

Suppose instead we determine to build our churches and shape our gospel discipleship around what the biblical text actually says, not on speculation. What kind of church would we build? The verses above would teach us to offer hospitality to one another, to share the gospel, to greet one another. All great things for Christians to do all week!

Further, we can examine the eight very clear, no-speculation-needed texts that describe the church of Corinth *gathering*:

1. "When you are assembled in the name of the Lord Jesus . . . deliver this man to Satan" (1 Cor. 5:4–5).
2. "When you come together as a church . . ." (1 Cor. 11:18; see also vv. 17 and 20).
3. "So then, my brothers, when you come together to eat, wait for one another" (1 Cor. 11:33; also v. 34).
4. "If, therefore, the whole church comes together and all speak in tongues, and outsiders or unbelievers enter . . ." (1 Cor. 14:23).
5. "Gaius, who is host to me and to the whole church, greets you." (Rom. 16:23).

I'm not sure how the Bible *could be clearer*. The Corinthian church in the singular gathers in the singular. Moreover, Corinth was a comparatively large city in the first-century Mediterranean world.

Further, each of these statements describes the activities that constitute a church as a church. In the first statement, Paul invokes the principle set forth in Matthew 18:20 ("where two or three are gathered in my name, there am I among them") when calling the church to exercise discipline. Discipline should not occur in an elder's meeting, a bishop's chair, or a small group; rather, "when you are assembled in the name of the Lord . . . with the power of our Lord Jesus . . ." (1 Cor. 5:4).

In the second and third statements, Paul ties the church gathering to the Lord's Supper. The fourth statement connects the church gathering to its corporate worship service. The fifth statement even tells us where the whole church met—in Gaius's house.

Speaking of the word "whole," people often use it to emphasize the entirety of something, in Greek as in English. Mark says, "And the whole city was gathered together at the door" (Mark 1:33). Does Mark envision multiple sub-cities coming together? Caiaphas refers to the "whole nation" perishing (John 11:50). Is he referring to an aggregation of subnations? In both cases one *could* argue that the word "whole" is redundant if the speakers didn't in fact have such an aggregation in mind. Yet the whole argument (by which I mean one argument, not an aggregation of separate arguments) would smack of special pleading, as does building a multisite church off of the word "whole."

So it is with the verses referring to the homes of Prisca and Aquilla, Titius Justus, Crispus, and so forth. You have to "plant the evidence" of a church in each text, because none of the texts confesses to it.

Traveling to Rome

We've seen enough of Corinth. Let's travel to Rome. What do we find? The first thing to notice is that we don't find what we found in Corinth: any reference to a singular church, as in "the church in Rome." Nowhere in Scripture do we find such a reference. Instead, Paul addresses the recipients of the letter as Christians: "To all those in Rome who are loved by God and called to be saints" (Rom. 1:7).

MUST A CHURCH MEET EVERY WEEK TO BE A CHURCH?

Multisite advocates sometimes argue that there is nothing in the New Testament to say that *all* the church must meet *every* week, but that quarterly, biannual, or annual meetings of all the church are just fine.* The trouble is that Scripture presents churches gathering weekly on the Lord's Day (e.g., 1 Cor. 16:2; cf. Rev. 1:10). Plus, the weekly cycle was hardwired not just into Israel's life but into creation itself. Where Israel worked six days and then rested on the seventh, Christians gather on the first day, resurrection day, indicating that we find our rest in Christ. He is our Sabbath. Then we work *out of that rest* for the next six days.

Weekly meetings impact a Christian's *daily* discipleship because the weekly cycle sets the regular rhythm for our daily lives and schedules. By contrast, I once served as a seminary trustee and attended meetings twice a year. I would see old friends, even share meals. But these meetings and relationships didn't affect my daily discipleship to Christ in any significant way.

The assembly with whom you gather weekly shapes your discipleship and keeps you accountable to Christ. Indeed, the first disciples "devoted themselves to the apostles' teaching and the fellowship" on a daily basis (Acts 2:42). They spent much time "attending the temple together" (v. 46). The author of Hebrews, too, exhorts us to "consider how to stir up one another to love and good works, not neglecting to meet together, as is the habit of some, but encouraging one another" (Heb. 10:24–25).

* J. D. Greear argues: "The question—our primary point of disagreement with 'single service only' advocates—is *whether the New Testament mandates that we must all assemble in the same place, at the same time, every week. . . .* We're committed to meeting altogether in *one* place at *one* time periodically throughout the

year—not every week, but on occasion—in fact, we assemble altogether about as often as ancient Israel did in its assembly. We think gathering all together, periodically, is an important expression of our assembly. . . . We believe the assembly of all people in the same place is a powerful encouragement to the body and compelling testimony to the world. But, we see nothing in the New Testament that demands that we assemble all together, every week, in the same place at the same time in one service." ("Is Multi-Site a Biblically Sound Model?," J. D. Greear Ministries, October 23, 2014, https://jdgreear.com/blog/multi-site-a-biblically-sound-model/).

That doesn't stop scholars from making assumptions. Gehring again: Paul "speaks, on the one hand, of the whole local church in Rom 1:7 (at least essentially even though not terminologically) and, on the other, of an individualization of this church as a whole in 16:5."[29] Gehring's phrase "essentially even though not terminologically" goes to the heart of why my own book must be written. Nowhere does Scripture say "church in Rome," but people want to view the word "church" as if it does. Gehring halfway concedes the point:

There does not appear . . . to be any evidence for a physical center for the house churches that were scattered through the city. Nowhere in the Letter to the Romans is the church as a whole in Rome called *ekklesia*, not even in 1:7, where it would normally be expected in a Pauline epistle. Nowhere is there mention that the local church in Rome gathered as a whole church in a citywide assembly.[30]

Still, he is confident 1:7 points to "one church," even though Paul doesn't say it.[31] I'm not sure why he's confident. For my part, I am not sure why we're even having the conversation at this point. Point to a hundred house churches in Rome. Fine. They are never connected together as one church.

Gehring's evidence for multiple house churches in Rome includes the following:[32]

- "Greet Prisca and Aquila, my fellow workers in Christ Jesus. . . . Greet also the church in their house" (Rom. 16:3, 5).
- "Greet Asyncritus, Phlegon, Hermes, Patrobas, Hermas, and the brothers who are with them" (16:14).
- "Greet Philologus, Julia, Nereus and his sister, and Olympas, and all the saints who are with them" (16:15).

Certainly the first refers to a house church. Perhaps the second and third do as well. I don't know, but the grouping of names who sound like family members and nonfamily members suggests it's plausible.

One matter worth noting is how, in the very next verse, Paul moves from second person back to third person: "Greet one another with a holy kiss. All the churches of Christ greet you" (16:16). If this were a modern-day letter, we would say Paul is not writing this letter to Prisca and the rest. He's telling the addressee to pass along his greetings to Prisca and the rest.

If the greetings of chapter 16 do in fact represent Paul's way of specially highlighting certain individuals and churches contained inside the "you" of this letter, then we should affirm, once again, that he's writing to all the Christians in Rome, as he says he is. He's not writing to one city church. He's writing to the Christians in Rome, spread across several churches. This is the explanation that requires the least speculation.

In fact, what occurs to me is how careful Paul is to *not* address "the church in Rome." He explicitly names the "church in Corinth" and then repeatedly refers to the Corinthians all gathering. In the letter to the Romans, however, he never names the church, and he never refers to all the Romans gathering. Instead, he mentions one house church and possibly alludes to a couple more. People talk about how flexibly Paul uses the term "church" when moving back and forth between citywide and house church. Actually, he's scrupulously careful. Comparing Corinth and Rome, the argument for multisite has to smother the details of both texts, albeit in opposite directions, in order to arrive at its conclusion.

A Brief Glance at Colossae and Laodicea

I hope you enjoyed Rome. Let's tour Colossae and Laodicea. As with the letter to the Romans, Paul does not address any Colossian church in the singular but writes to "the saints and faithful brothers in Christ at Colossae" (1:2). His letter to Philemon, who lived in Colossae, tells us that a church met in Philemon's house: "To Philemon ... and the church in your house" (Philem. 1–2). So either there was one church in Colossae, and they met in Philemon's house, or there were multiple churches, one meeting in his house and others meeting elsewhere. However you look at it, there's nothing to suggest a multisite church.

Toward the end of his letter to the Colossians, Paul says: "Give my greetings to the brothers at Laodicea, and to Nympha and the church in her house. And when this letter has been read among you, have it also read in the church of the Laodiceans; and see that you also read the letter from Laodicea" (Col. 4:15–16). Gehring tells us Laodicea was 9.3 miles away from Colossae, which may be a short commute in freeway miles, but was a little more in those days. He further explains that "the house church of Nympha is probably in Laodicea," which does not seem entirely unreasonable, since verse 15 begins with the Laodiceans, mentions the church in her house, and then returns to the Laodiceans in verse 16. Plus, Paul clearly mentions two churches: the church in Nympha's house and the Laodiceans, and the church of the Laodiceans "is most likely not identical with Nympha's house church."[33]

Gehring then draws the pieces together: "If Nympha's house church can be located in Laodicea, we would have a house church within the overall local church in that area."[34]

It's a reasonable conjecture. It's hypothetically possible. Maybe Nympha's house church gathers quarterly with the larger church. Maybe they share a common "vision, budget, leadership, and board" with the larger church. Then again, it's just that: conjecture. The text says none of these things. It suggests in no way that the one congregation is part of the larger church. It refers to one church, and then to another church. Period. The easiest explanation would seem to be that there are two churches.

Going House to House in Jerusalem

We could keep traveling city by city. But the trip works just as easily in the form of a self-guided tour. Write on one page all the occurrences of the word "church" for Thessalonica as well as anything that speaks to a gathering or sounds like a house church. Don't forget to use Acts. Then try Philippi, and Ephesus, and Cenchreae, and so forth. For each destination, don't *look* for a multisite church, as if it's hiding behind the biblical text and only an arm or foot is exposed—"Well, that *could* be . . ." Look at what the text says, and then describe what you see.[35]

Yet let's complete the guided portion of our tour in Jerusalem. It's a little more complicated, so I can understand why some, with a quick glance, would conclude, "The very first Christian church was a multisite church."[36] On the one hand, Luke explicitly refers to one church when he says "the whole church" as well as "the church in Jerusalem" (Acts 5:11; 8:1). As in Corinth, he also describes the whole church gathering together a number of times:

- ". . . attending the temple *together*" (Acts 2:46).
- "And they were *all together* in Solomon's Portico" (Acts 5:12).
- "And the twelve summoned *the full number* of the disciples" (Acts 6:2).

On the other hand, Luke offers a clear record of house-to-house fellowship.

- "And day by day, attending the temple together and breaking bread *in their homes*, they received their food with glad and generous hearts" (Acts 2:46).
- "And every day, in the temple and *from house to house*, they did not cease teaching and preaching that the Christ is Jesus" (Acts 5:42; cf. 20:20).

- "But Saul was ravaging the church, and entering *house after house*, he dragged off men and women and committed them to prison" (Acts 8:3).
- "[Peter] went to *the house* of Mary . . . where many were gathered together and were praying" (Acts 12:12).

For these reasons, Brad House and Gregg Allison argue that the church of Jerusalem is distributed across various houses: "The Bible tells us that the church of Jerusalem gathered together in the temple, *and* the church of Jerusalem gathered together in homes."[37] In the temple, say House and Allison, "the apostles preached and performed signs and wonders, and the believers enjoyed fellowship, gave sacrificially, worshipped, and prayed." In the homes, "the Word was preached, prayers were voiced, money was given sacrificially, the Lord's Supper was celebrated, and more, the church of Jerusalem assembled to worship." They punctuate this last point: "The church—not the churches—of Jerusalem gathered in these many locations."[38]

Gehring offers a slightly different nomenclature: "The primitive church in Jerusalem came together in the temple in a large meeting as the *whole church*, and in private homes as individual church bodies as *house churches*."[39] Still, the division of labor between the two kinds of locations is roughly the same. Either way, should we therefore say that the very first church, the church in Jerusalem, was a multisite church?

I might be convinced if there were no record of the entire Jerusalem church gathering and doing churchy things like preaching and baptism (see Acts 2:41). Imagine an alternative version of Acts where *all you have* are these house-to-house gatherings with preaching and baptism and the Supper, *and yet the text still refers to the "church in Jerusalem."* Okay, I'd say. That's a multisite church. As the book of Acts reads, however, the whole Jerusalem church regularly (daily?) gathers.

My church—singular—also meets from house to house. We call those meetings "small groups." My own small group meets on

Wednesday night at the Broggis' house. Other churches call them "community groups." Most don't need to call them anything, because this is what Christians *do*. Christians in healthy churches meet in one another's homes for fellowship, Bible study, sometimes singing, hospitality, and more throughout the week. Sometimes it's scheduled; often it's spontaneous. Yet what *makes* a church a church, among other things, is that its members all meet together on Sunday—minus anyone who is sick, traveling, homebound, or otherwise unable to attend. So it was with the church in Jerusalem. They all met together.

IS THE "CHURCH" REALLY GATHERING IF MEMBERS ARE SICK, TRAVELING, OR SERVING IN CHILDCARE?

Multisite advocates sometimes respond to the arguments for one assembly with a reductio ad absurdum: "If the whole church needs to assemble for the church to be a church, what about members who are sick, traveling, or working in childcare?"

Once again, the critique misses what ultimately makes a church: it's not the presence of every member but the fact that Jesus says he's present with the gathering. If thirty members of a thirty-five-member church are present, Jesus is still there, sealing their gathering with his authority.

To keep insisting the Jerusalem church is a multisite church, therefore, suggests one of two things. Either you've been a part of churches where members treat church as a Sunday-only thing, so that you're surprised by the house-to-house fellowships in Acts and you conclude they must be churches. Or you have an underdeveloped conception of what a gathering is and what role a gathering plays in making a church a church.

The latter is the more obvious conclusion. Multisite advocates, by their very name, don't believe a gathering or assembly is an essential part of making a church a church. They haven't given due consideration to what the thrice-mentioned "whole church" gathering in Jerusalem *means* or *does* or *accomplishes*. After all, if you believe that two campuses can never meet and still constitute one "church," then you don't think a gathering is a necessary element for making a church a church. You might insist the people gather somewhere. Fine. But *the multisite church itself* is an "assembly" that never assembles, a "gathering" that never gathers, a "church" that never churches.

A question to ask multisiters is What role *does* a gathering play in a church becoming a church? It's not clear to me that everyone who affirms the multisite or multiservice structure has considered this question.

House and Allison have called my argument that the multisite church removes the assembly from the assembly a "hypercriticism." They say it rests on the "methodological error of defining a concept by the word." For instance, we wouldn't say "salvation" in the Bible means *only* an act of saving or that "justification" means *only* the act of justifying, they reason. No, the concepts are much larger than that.

It's true that being "saved" from sin and death is not the same things as being "saved" from a fashion faux pas by an attentive wife. We need more than dictionaries to do theology. Certainly. But is there a form of salvation that doesn't involve saving? Or justification that doesn't involve justifying? The actual use of a word usually involves *more* than the dictionary definition of a word, but *less*? I can picture different kinds of assemblies. I have a hard time envisioning an assembly that doesn't assemble.

Yet multisiters do indeed propose a use of "assembly" (*ekklēsia*) that doesn't involve assembling. The separate assemblies assemble, yes. But the one big thing multisiters call a "church" *doesn't actually assemble*, at least not of necessity. And if the Greek word for "church" is "assembly," it would seem we have an assembly that doesn't assemble.

Before we leave Jerusalem, there is one more passage to notice. It's this one from Acts 2:

> And they devoted themselves to the apostles' teaching and the fellowship, to the breaking of bread and the prayers. And awe came upon every soul, and many wonders and signs were being done through the apostles. And all who believed were together and had all things in common. And they were selling their possessions and belongings and distributing the proceeds to all, as any had need. And day by day, attending the temple together and breaking bread in their homes, they received their food with glad and generous hearts, praising God and having favor with all the people. And the Lord added to their number day by day those who were being saved. (vv. 42–47)

The question this passage poses is this: Do the references to "the breaking of bread" in verse 42 and "breaking bread in their homes" in verse 46 suggest the people were receiving the Lord's Supper in their homes, as House and Allison argue? And, if so, doesn't that mean the Jerusalem church (singular) was exercising the church sign and seal of the Supper in its members' homes?

What's difficult is that the noun phrase "the breaking of bread" and the verbal phrase "breaking bread" can refer to an ordinary meal[40] or to the consecrated meal that we regard as the Lord's Supper.[41] So which of the two is in mind in verses 42 and 46? Commentators debate the structure of these verses. Is verse 42 listing the basic elements of a liturgy? Is it functioning instead as a heading for the verses that follow, which describe the church both in its gathered and scattered capacity? Or are verses 46 and 47 functioning as a summary for everything that preceded?

I don't think we need to nail down answers to those questions. I think this much is clear: the paragraph envisions the Jerusalem church in both its gathered liturgical capacity and its scattered, everyday-life capacity. The people are gathering in the temple for the formal activities of worship. And they're scattering to each other's home to share all of life together. Whether verse 42, then, is referring to the Lord's Supper or not, I genuinely don't know but don't think it makes any difference for my argument. Ancient Near Eastern temples, mind you, were something like the restaurants of the day. People would come to eat all the sacrificed meat (hence, you have Paul's extended discussions on eating meat sacrificed to idols in 1 Cor. 9 and Rom. 14). It's entirely possible that the Jerusalem church practiced the Lord's Supper together in Solomon's Colonnade. Obviously, the text doesn't say that, but nor does it say where they *did* celebrate the Supper. After all, Acts 2:46 seems to refer to ordinary meals: "Breaking bread in their homes, they received their food with glad and generous hearts." Their generous hearts are sharing food, and people are gladly receiving it. Why? Verse 45 tell us that some "had need." They were glad, presumably, because it was food and people were hungry.

Yet, even if I'm mistaken and verse 46 does refer to the Lord's Supper, my primary interest here remains a lexical one about whether the word "church" is ever used in the New Testament for something that does not regularly gather. And it is beyond dispute that the Jerusalem church gathered all together in the temple for preaching and baptism (Acts 2:1, 6). The house-to-house gatherings, furthermore, are wonderful and expected expressions of the church living out its life through the week. It's impossible to conclude that the *ekklēsia* in Jerusalem is an assembly that doesn't assemble. The Jerusalem church, clearly, assembles. So does the *ekklēsia* in Corinth. The gatherings in Rome, on the other hand, never gather as one *ekklēsia*, and they are never named as one *ekklēsia*.

We could go through city after city. The burden of proof is on the multisiters to demonstrate that the New Testament's usage departs radically from Jewish and Greco-Roman usage. It certainly evolves some, such that *ekklēsia* can stand in for the *dēmos*. I simply don't see anything concrete to suggest it drops the *ekklēsia* from the *ekklēsia* entirely.

The lesson remains: an assembly must assemble to be an assembly.

Conclusion

I'm not a Greek scholar. But at the risk of punching above my weight class, I propose that a good Greek lexicon should include both the local church and the universal church in order to represent Scripture accurately, and the local church is something that gathers. Remember, these assemblies are earthly, in-time outposts of a glorious heavenly and eschatological reality. Indeed, the reason New Testament authors can refer to the scattered church as "assembly" is that its reality is rooted in something even more basic and primary, namely, the future heavenly assembly. We must never read the term "assembly" in the *already* apart from the *not yet*. The *already* entails the *not yet*. Yet, if the assembly never assembles, how can it be a sign of the *not yet*? After all, the *not yet* assembles.

3

A CHURCH SHOULD
BE CATHOLIC

The argument of this book has been that multisite and multiservice churches repudiate the Bible's definition of a church as a single assembly, redefine the church, and reshape it morally. The models pick a fight with Jesus, I said in the introduction. I have attempted to make this case in chapters 1 and 2 by examining how Jesus defines a church (chap. 1) and then demonstrating how the apostles never break from Jesus's definition (chap. 2). Anything that breaks from Jesus's definition is that repudiation, redefinition, and reshaping.

The last thing to talk about is alternatives to multiple services or sites. Wonderfully, this continues the biblical discussion. The Bible calls churches to work together. In fact, what the introduction called the Bible's ontological and moral mandate for churches to remain one assembly forces them to work together. A full building is a kind of healthy disruption. It requires a church to think less of its own ministry and more of the ministry of the kingdom, sort of like the persecution in the early chapters of Acts forcing the Jerusalem church outward.

No doubt, a full building is a good problem to have. Thank God for it. Still, the question has to be answered: Now what?

The first obvious solution is to build a bigger meeting space. Christians sometimes think of this as poor stewardship, but such a reaction might be a bit shortsighted. Way back in 1911 several hundred saints with far less disposable income than most Americans have today sacrificed to build the brick structure where the Capitol Hill Baptist Church has met ever since. And since 1911, how many sermons have been preached, how many saints edified, how many children and non-Christian neighbors saved, how many missionaries have been sent, how many poor cared for? For over a century Christians and non-Christians have been blessed. I would say that amounts to pretty good stewardship on the part of those older saints.

But okay. Building a larger building is not always feasible, and there are plenty of reasons why it might not be the best option in any given circumstance.

Plus, there is a much more significant matter at stake behind the topic of alternatives, and that's our catholicity—our recognition of other churches—or lack thereof. Working with other churches is perhaps the most crucial, promising, natural, and biblical alternative to the multiple-site-or-service model. This might mean planting, revitalizing, peaceably dividing, or just encouraging attendees to join a church closer to where they live. Yet, being convinced of this alternative depends on possessing strong catholic instincts, which many church leaders today lack. It depends upon giving up control, which is hard for us.

DISTINGUISHING LITTLE C FROM BIG C CATHOLIC

Most people associate the word "catholic" with the Roman Catholic Church. Yet, when used with a little *c*, the word simply means worldwide or universal. This is why Protestants use the Nicene Creed to affirm their belief in the "one, holy, catholic, apostolic church."

Therefore, that's where we need to begin. It's not enough to list the alternatives to the multisite model. Our church intuitions need to become more catholic—more appreciative of our partnership with other churches.

Are Your Intuitions Catholic?

Let me illustrate. A multisite megachurch in the suburbs of a medium-sized city decided they wanted to reach the students of the city's downtown university. What a great idea!

To this end, they decided to plant a "campus" of their church two blocks away from the university's campus. Incidentally, that put them literally next door to my friend Greg's church. Greg is an excellent preacher. His church has been growing steadily—some might say quickly—through his tenure. It's even Southern Baptist, just like the megachurch.

Yet, for one reason or another, the megachurch never contacted Greg. They never asked how they could support his ministry or even how they could partner in doing ministry together. They just showed up next door—a vessel of the suburban mothership.

Does that strike you as strange? It might not, because it's fairly normal today. It's what churches today do. Reach capacity? Start another service. Want to reach another neighborhood? Plant a campus.

Yet imagine the New Testament apostles advising this megachurch to act as they did:

Paul, an apostle, to the church in *suburban* Corinth, grace and peace to you.

We hear news of an opportunity to share the love of God in Christ to the college students of Corinth. Don't concern yourselves with the saints who already live next to their school. Plant a group of yourselves there. I know all too well the brother and sisters in the church at Corinth. They are troubled by a host of matters. Ignore them, lest their programming preferences hinder your proven formula.

The grand irony, of course, is that multisite advocates argue that the actual church in Corinth consisted of multiple house churches working together as one church, which these advocates use as an excuse, apparently, to plant their own campuses so that they *don't have to work together with other churches in their city but can overlook them.*

I dare say there is a quiet undercurrent of disunity in this megachurch's approach, as well as in the multisite model generally, even if they support other churches in other ways.

Think of Paul criticizing those who say, "I follow Paul" or "I follow Apollos" or "I follow Cephas" (1 Cor. 1:12). He believed the Corinthians put too much confidence in these men, which led to quarreling. The megachurch in my illustration didn't outwardly quarrel with Greg's church. It ignored his church. I don't know why. Let's assume good motives ("We want to reach students"; "We want to maximize our resources"). Still, I propose there was too much *independence* in their thinking and not enough *interdependence*, not enough catholicity. And that lack of catholicity, that overexuberant independence, is its own kind of divisiveness or factionalism, relative to other churches like Greg's. Even with good motives, the foundational assumption of such independence is a trust in ourselves and the things under our control, combined with a reluctance to trust God's ability to work through other churches. Such independence, in other words, is finally a faith issue.

I don't blame just the megachurch for this. That's the Christian landscape today and an indictment of what seems natural or inevitable to all of us. It's our church intuitions, as I've been saying. We just don't think about working with other churches. Whether multisite or single-site, congregational or episcopal, we think instead about our own church's programs, growth, and health.

Ask yourself:

- Do I regularly pray publicly for other churches in my city?
- Have we ever supported them financially with overages in our church budget?

- Does my church website list other nearby churches that we would recommend? (One church I know of has a "Sister Churches" webpage on its site.)
- Do we have a brochure at the building's entrance listing those churches? (The abovementioned church does this as well.)
- If a pastor, have I ever found myself saying in a church-membership interview, "We'd love to have you here, but have you ever thought about joining Grace Church? They're a mile or two from your house, not thirty minutes away, like we are."
- Do I meet regularly with other pastors in my city to strategize together or encourage one another?
- Do I discipline myself to speak well of other churches, and warn only when necessary, and with great care?
- Does our church plan gospel outreach events with other churches?

Or here's a doozy that my friend Andy once preached: if you pray for revival and it comes to the church down the street, do you rejoice?[1] (There's a clear alternative to multisite: pray for revival in the other guy's church.)

Getting Catholic

What I'm saying is that we need to get more catholic—meaning, we need a more developed sense of our partnership with churches everywhere.

I'm not saying we should build authoritatively binding connections between them, like placing a bishop over multiple churches. That's one mistake of everyone from the worldwide Roman Catholic Church to the countrywide German Lutheran Church to the citywide multisite church. We are new covenant Christians. Therefore, authority remains with people who can literally shake hands in agreement with one another because they are gathered together, as I argued in chapter 2. Born-again hearts don't need global structures or city structures. But they do need a global and city mindset, one that both affirms God's work through other churches and shapes how we do ministry. We're not "on mission" on behalf of our own local churches. We're "on mission" on behalf of Christ's kingdom, and our churches are outposts of it. We fight for it together. We belong to the same team. We share the same family name. We are one in faith, baptism, and mission. And the New Testament affirms that partnership.

From the very beginning, New Testament churches worked together. Acts starts with the church in Jerusalem. Then another church shows up—the church in Antioch. Did they ignore each other? By no means. A "great number" of Greeks came to faith, and so the apostles sent Barnabas to investigate and to strengthen these new believers (Acts 11:21–24). The church in Antioch, in turn, learned about the famine and hardship coming upon the believers in Judea, leading them to send aid by Barnabas and Saul (vv. 27–30). These churches recognized their partnership together.

We could keep reading in Acts or walk through the Epistles to see the same thing: churches recognized their common cause and worked together. Consider how they shared love and greetings:

- "All the churches of Christ greet you" (Rom. 16:16).
- "The churches of Asia send you greetings" (1 Cor. 16:19).
- "I have heard of your faith in the Lord Jesus and your love toward all the saints" (Eph. 1:15; also 2 Cor. 13:13; Eph. 6:22; Col. 1:4).

They shared preachers and missionaries:

- "With him we are sending the brother who is famous among all the churches for his preaching of the gospel" (2 Cor. 8:18).
- "Beloved, it is a faithful thing you do in all your efforts for these brothers, strangers as they are, who testified to your love before the church" (3 John 5–6a).

They imitated one another in Christian living:

- "You became an example to all the believers in Macedonia and in Achaia" (1 Thess. 1:7).
- "For you, brothers, became imitators of the churches of God in Christ Jesus that are in Judea" (1 Thess. 2:14).

They supported one another financially with joy and thanksgiving:

- "At present, however, I am going to Jerusalem bringing aid to the saints. For Macedonia and Achaia have been pleased to make some contribution for the poor among the saints at Jerusalem" (Rom. 15:25–26).
- "For the ministry of this service is not only supplying the needs of the saints but is also overflowing in many thanksgivings to God" (2 Cor. 9:12; also 2 Cor. 8:1–2).

Indeed, Paul instructed them to care for one another financially:

- "Now concerning the collection for the saints: as I directed the churches of Galatia, so you also are to do. On the first day of every week, each of you is to put something aside and store it up, as he may prosper, so that there will be no collecting when I come. And when I arrive, I will send those whom you accredit by letter to carry your gift to Jerusalem" (1 Cor. 16:1–3).
- "So give proof before the churches of your love and of our boasting about you to these men" (2 Cor. 8:24).

He also exhorted them to pray for other churches and Christians:

- "To that end, keep alert with all perseverance, making supplication for all the saints" (Eph. 6:18).

In short, the New Testament teaches that the Great Commission is bigger than our churches.[2] Sadly, many churches today go it alone, like the megachurch that planted a church next to Greg's.

Let me use another illustration. Imagine you belong to a battalion of Allied soldiers charged with pushing an enemy out of an occupied Belgian city. Your battalion of eight hundred soldiers consists of four companies of two hundred soldiers each. But your own company commander decides *not* to work with the three other companies. He's confident in his strategy alone. Step 1: divide his company into four parts. Step 2: dispatch the four parts to different parts of the city (which means your company will stumble over the other three companies). Step 3: cheer the four parts forward by reminding them they are "one company."

It's not difficult to envision how this approach will divide and frustrate the work of the battalion, even if your company commander is wildly talented in comparison to the other three. You will move into the same neighborhoods in an uncoordinated fashion. You and your fellow company members will identify with the company more than with the battalion. Your company officers will make decisions that favor your company, even if making sacrifices for another company would help the battalion. And the battalion's offensive into the city will suffer.

Turning to churches, I am not suggesting we should unite all the churches in a city under one leadership in a battalion structure. I am saying we need a battalion *mind-set*, even while we fight through our individual companies, or churches. This is part of what it means to live inside an "already–not yet" eschatology. All the structures of Christ's global rule will become visible in glory, but the global (battalion) mind-set should characterize us now. Our churches are outposts of Christ's kingdom. Our local bodies are expressions of *the* body, of *the* church. Church leaders especially must know this and keep a comparatively loose grip on their own programs. They must know deep in their bones, as Mark Dever puts it, that the doors of their churches might close, but *the* church will be just fine. Why? Because Christ has promised as much. And that knowledge should guide our programming and structural decisions.

Contrast this kingdom mentality with the vibe one feels at the friend of a friend's church. I'll call it New Life. The pastors on stage continually address the congregation as "New Lifers," not as brothers and sisters in Christ. They constantly refer to their church by name: "We here at New Life like to . . ." or "New Life is all about . . ." They almost sound like sales managers training a new sales force, cultivating a sense of team identity and commitment by repeating the company name over and over.

Mind you, I have spent the better part of my professional career trying to help Christians commit themselves more fully to their own local churches. Don't say you follow Jesus if all you have is a vague commitment to the church everywhere. But! Our membership in the assembly of heaven comes first.

Church leader, are you as interested in promoting the kingdom of Christ as you are your own church's program?

Getting catholic and working with other churches means making sacrifices and losing control. For instance, you sacrifice members by sending them to help the struggling church one neighborhood over. Or you lose control by sending out a church plant instead of planting a campus. All this takes faith that God works through other churches just as he works through yours.

So picture that moment that began this book: you're trying to help visitors find seats, but the room is full. They walk back into the hallway and sit on the hallway bench. Maybe they leave. Does this incident make you think, "We *have* to add a second service"?

I have lived through such moments. I've seen and felt that frustration myself. I have had friends tell me they spent twenty minutes looking for parking on Sunday morning and eventually left. If the previous two chapters of this book are correct and Scripture intends for churches to exist as one assembly, it takes faith in these moments to trust: "The kingdom of Christ does not depend upon my church. God can and will use other churches in those people's lives. Their salvation or growth in the faith does not depend on changing the DNA of a church to accommodate them."

Just think of the church in Jerusalem scattering as a result of persecution. Did that ultimately help or hurt the church's mission? The members of the Jerusalem church may have preferred to remain comfortably in one place, but God knew it was time to send them out. He meant for them to spread.

Ironically, recognizing how the Bible confines a church to one time in one space forces that church to spread when it becomes full. The inconveniences of fullness serves an outward-launching evangelistic purpose. Full buildings serve a missional purpose.

Faith, after all, involves long-term instead of short-term thinking. Short-term thinking says, "We have to do whatever it takes this Sunday." Long-term faith recognizes that some compromises we make this Sunday actually hurt our mission in the long run. It believes that fifteen single-service churches in a city, all things being equal, are better for the Great Commission than five three-service-or-site churches. Yes, this even includes the people turned away on any given Sunday. They will eventually benefit from the strength and health that one-assembly churches offer over and against multisite and multiservice churches, again, all other things being equal. Catholicity, in short, requires faith—faith in God's work through other churches and faith in his work over time.

As Westerners, we assume that our church must never be hindered from growing numerically. We assume we must accommodate infinite growth. To do otherwise would not be evangelistic.

The trouble with this assumption is the un-catholic "we." It's true that "we" can never stop growing, but only because "we" includes all the gospel-preaching churches in your city and in the world. "You," on the other hand, can stop growing because "we" is bigger than "you."

Being content to stop adding to the roll when the room is full doesn't mean you care about the kingdom less; it means you'll pursue growth differently now, like the athlete who wins the gold medal and then turns to coaching others to do the same.

Catholicity means you are as interested in helping others win gold medals as you are in winning them yourself.

Referral and Partnership

So what are the alternatives to multiple services and sites? I mentioned building a bigger building at the beginning of the chapter. That may or may not be a viable option, depending on location and other resources.

Yet, per the conversation on catholicity, the easiest, most effective, and probably the most important alternative is learning how to work with other churches. It's referral and partnership. You have to squint your eyes, tilt your head, and make a host of assumptions to find multisite churches in the biblical text. Meanwhile, the catholic argument for working with other churches is as crystal clear in Scripture as all the bullet points listed in the previous section. How strange it is that we forsake what's concrete in the Bible for something speculative.

I've already mentioned a few practical ways to begin this process: list trusted nearby churches on your website; print that list on a brochure and place it near the doors of the church building; ask visitors if they've considered a particular church closer to their home; plan outreach events with other churches; speak well of other churches; invite other pastors to share about their churches in your prayer service; pray privately and publicly for nearby churches weekly; avoid program-recruitment language ("Good morning, New Lifers!"), but use biblical language instead ("brothers and sisters," "saints"). We could keep going: cooperate with other churches in sending missionaries and supporting seminary students; provide pulpit supply for other churches, or ask for it; and so on.

Investing in Other Pastors

But more than any list of concrete suggestions for how to partner and refer, a pastor needs to get his head around this: part of his job description includes investing in other pastors and promoting the

TRANSITIONS AND OTHER IRREGULARITIES

Deciding what to label a "church" in the real world is a little messier than defining one on paper. Suppose a church building burns down, and, while rebuilding, the congregation meets for a year in a smaller structure that divides them in half. Do the two assemblies remain one church or temporarily become two? Or suppose a church "incubates" a church plant with a second site or service for a brief season. The "mother church" maintains some measure of authority over the new site or second service, all the while gradually transferring authority. When does that second site or service become its own church?

The birth of any new and independent organization, team, family, battalion, club, or other corporate entity typically requires a time of transition. During that transition, furthermore, some of the regular rules or realities don't apply in a straightforward fashion. A man leaves his father and mother for college. At some point they stop paying for his rent, then his car insurance, then his phone bill. Eventually they stop declaring him as a "dependent" on their taxes, and he pays his own. Then he unites to a wife and has children. Somewhere through that whole process we call him an "adult" and the US Census Bureau decides he's his own "household."

Likewise, becoming a church in the real world, and not on paper, happens in stages. In fact, we see this kind of organizational flexibility on the pages of Acts, as when baptisms occur outside the context of local churches (e.g., Acts 8:26–39; 16:13–15, 29–33). (We don't, ironically, see such flexibility in how the term "church" is used, despite claims to the contrary.) This is the nature of a growing missionary religion, particularly a religion that defines itself through its assemblies. Those assemblies must undergo cell division, one outpost becoming two, two becoming four, and so forth. But that division and growth doesn't always happen the same way or with the "click" of a light switch.

Put simply, talking about church organization requires us to draw from two buckets: biblical regularities and circumstantial irregularities. For instance, a church with no pastors is still a church (as in Acts 14:23 or Titus 1:5). It's simply an irregular church. It doesn't conform to the "regula" (which means "rule" in Latin) of Scripture. Therefore, that church should work to get pastors. Likewise, a church temporarily divided between two services because its building burned down, or because it's incubating a church plant, is an irregular church. It should work itself back toward regularity, back toward the regula or rule of Scripture with one assembly.

If a church cannot gather weekly due to some type of constraint, it should begin the sometimes slow task of peaceably dividing into separate churches—for the sake of kingdom advancement and gain.

health of other churches. We see that exemplified in the "catholic" texts above (p. 103). We learn it from Paul's charge to Timothy "What you have heard from me in the presence of many witnesses entrust to faithful men, who will be able to teach others also" (2 Tim. 2:2). Yes, that charge at least applies to teaching men in one's own congregation, but nothing in the text limits it to that.

When Mark Dever arrived at Capitol Hill Baptist Church in late 1994, one of his first tasks was to acquaint himself with other nearby pastors—Baptist, Presbyterian, Anglican, Lutheran, and more. A few were theologically conservative; most were liberal. He also began attending meetings of the DC Baptist Convention. Within a few years, it became evident the DCBC had been overwhelmed by theological liberalism. So he withdrew and started his own Columbia Baptist Ministers' Association. At first, three or four pastors from the area attended, then a few more, and now forty or so attend. These brothers meet monthly for lunch at one church. An assistant brings Subway sandwiches. They discuss books they have been reading together. They compare church budgets so they might learn from one another. They give each other counsel on tough pastoral-care cases. And so forth. No authority structure binds them, but the partnership does: "Can someone supply me with a preacher for my two weeks of vacation this summer?" "How did you guys decide which missionaries to support?" "We just discovered our church treasurer has been stealing from us and not been paying our taxes. We owe a huge amount of back taxes, together with penalties. We're desperate." Pastoral fellowship is critical for building catholic-mindedness and Great Commission purposefulness.

Attractional versus Catholic Church Cultures

Yet partnership and referral depend upon a whole church's culture, too. Attractional churches tend to lack catholic sensibilities, at least in terms of giving attention to other churches. Attractional churches may celebrate the work of the universal church around the world, but the continual rehearsal of their mission and vision statements and the continual promotional language about what *their* church is doing tends to detract, even if unintentionally, from partnering with and referring to other churches in their area. Consider, for instance, how many smaller churches were swallowed up by attractional megachurches in the 1980s, '90s, and 2000s in so many American cities. Attractional and catholic sensibilities typically, if unintentionally, work at cross purposes.

Let me unpack this. The basic evangelistic instinct of an attractional mentality is to draw people into a church by emphasizing relevance and sameness. They say, in effect, "We have the solutions to the problems you feel. We are not scary but down-to-earth and fun-loving like you. We won't talk about the gospel as a judicial summons from a holy God; rather, we'll talk about all the good things you've been looking for like purpose, wholeness, good marriages, the abundant life." Which means—and this is crucial—attractional churches tend to build on brand, aesthetics, and personality. Like the marketplace generally, the goal is to *attract*. And such ministries consciously and deliberately seek to attract people with the same things the marketplace does: good parking, good music, good coffee, charming personalities, a distinct brand. If you think I'm overstating it, read the church-growth books.

Now, this isn't all bad. People come. But there are unintended consequences. For instance, the devices of the marketplace aren't exactly conducive to encouraging people to eat in another guy's restaurant. You'll never see a McDonald's commercial celebrating their common cause with Burger King in solving the problem of hunger.[3]

For example, why does every young church planter these days feel compelled to articulate a "mission statement" and a "vision statement," which will then be regularly rehearsed on stage, in videos, and in all the church's literature? If you had asked pastors for the first two thousand years of church history what their mission statement was, they would have looked confused by the question and then probably opened their Bibles and pointed to the last verses of Matthew 28. I don't doubt that pastors today *mean* for their mission and vision statements to teach and remind their members of who they are and what God calls us to do. But the medium is the message, and what those statements simultaneously *do* is distinguish *their* church from *the other guy's* church.

I still remember the Burger King commercials in my childhood emphasizing the fact that, unlike McDonalds, its burgers were "flame broiled" (though I just learned in a Google search that the company decided in 2003 to change their brand to "fire grilled"). Likewise, I could cite several key phrases right now—I won't—that you could identify with certain prominent churches. Those phrases pack in good messages, yes, but they also fix our attention on them, that church, those pastors, their ministry. They are subtly anti-catholic, because church brand management, of which mission and vision statements are a piece, is implicitly anti-catholic.

Should it surprise anyone that multiservice and multisite structures have become popular in the era of commercialism? They fit hand in glove, even when multisite pastors sincerely have better than commercialistic intentions.

Yet, now picture an alternative universe, one where these talent-filled, resource-rich megachurches use their talents and resources not to emphasize their programs and their brands but exclusively to supply and equip their members *as well as other trusted churches*. Perhaps the last forty years would have been characterized not by their swallowing up so many smaller churches but by their strengthening them. Perhaps our cities would have fewer powerhouse megachurches that people drive forty-five minutes to attend, but instead would boast many more vibrant small and medium-sized churches living the Christian life together like families.

I'm not saying smaller churches are necessarily better. Nor am I saying all preachers are equally gifted. God hasn't created all pastors and churches to be "gold medalists." Some surely are, and let's rejoice over that fact. Yet the most productive pastors are those just as interested in helping others onto the medal stand, and that involves more than writing a book to tell others how to do what you did. It involves the structures and ministries of your church, because your church is more powerful than you—at least it should be. It also involves a lifestyle of quiet, behind-the-curtain service and promotion of others.

If you want to convince a good number of multisite churches to abandon that structure, you'll have to first convince them to abandon their attractional mind-set and to adopt a catholic one instead (the same lesson applies for single-site pastors). A post-multisite world probably requires a post-attractional world.

To mention a better example, I think of the church of my pastor friend Aaron. Originally his elders listed "planting another church" as a five-year goal. But as they thought and prayed, that slowly morphed into "building a culture of serving other churches." They shared this vision with the congregation, which energized them to begin praying and looking for ways to serve other churches right away. It also helped the church prepare for planting down the road.

Training Leaders and Teachers

Another crucial piece of developing catholic-mindedness is promoting pastoral and leadership development inside one's church. The point here is that churches should learn to see the value of many leaders rather than just one leader, because ultimately it's the word of God they value, not one man's way of preaching the word. Plus, as a church trains more and more leaders, some of those leaders will leave and take members with them—a success! It's the geographic expansion of the kingdom. Leadership training serves catholicity, which increases our ability to trust and work with other churches.

On a number of occasions, I've heard a multisite pastor or a member of his staff explain that the church strongly favors his preaching. The church is as large as it is because people come for him. I assume this is true. Some really are gold medalists. Suppose, however, that this gold-medalist preacher decided to preach only half the year. This would simultaneously give other men the opportunity to grow while also helping the church to value God's word more than the man. It would prepare the church for plants and revitalization efforts (see below, p. 117). Add to this efforts by the church to create many more teaching opportunities in Sunday school classrooms and small groups and prayer services and so on. Little by little that church will build up a stockpile of gifted teachers, some of whom will leave and bless other churches.

In short, a post-multisite world is most likely a post-building-a-church-on-one-preacher world, because catholicity and a multitude of teachers work hand in hand. To be sure, many multisite churches work hard at raising up a plurality of elders and teachers.

Praise God. Yet, beyond that, their lead men should also consider how they might hold themselves back in order to push others forward—focus on coaching other medalists, even if it means removing themselves from an event or two. Sometimes Jesus preached. Sometimes he withdrew. Sometimes he sent out the seventy-two in his stead. I'm not saying he intended to offer us a model for our churches in doing that, but I do think we can learn from it.

The Value of Geographic Proximity

Pastors should teach their congregations to understand the significance of geographic proximity. Incidentally, this is a matter that one-assembly and multisite pastors will agree on relative to the multiservice pastor. Yet, where the multisite apologist uses the significance of geographic proximity as a reason to unite a number of churches in a city under the label of "one church," the lesson is better used to promote catholicity and partnering with other churches.

Specifically, the lesson is this: the church can most easily be the church when members join congregations near their homes, or move to homes near the church meeting place. It's easier to disciple you when you live on my block, and easier for our wives to enjoy fellowship. And together the four of us can evangelize and care for our neighbors. Developing these sensibilities, in turn, helps Christians understand why they might not want to drive thirty minutes to the megachurch, and why the 150-member church a few minutes from their home might actually do more for their discipleship and evangelism, assuming they also work at building relationships in that place.

What should be clear from this discussion is that finding alternatives to multiple services or sites requires much more than pointing to bigger buildings, church plants, or anything else. It generally depends on an overall way of being the church and doing ministry. It depends on a thousand small decisions and conversations that train the church and its leaders to value the kinds of partnership exemplified in the New Testament.

In this environment you can envision yourself saying to the visitor who cannot find a seat on Sunday: "I'm so sorry. We are frustratingly full. I hope you'll try again, but if you're discouraged from doing so, here's a list of five other excellent churches who preach the Bible as well as, if not better than, we do." And in this environment the family who loves the lead preacher's preaching isn't so dependent on that preacher that they cannot envision leaving as part of a church plant.

Church Plants and Revitalizations

Here's an interesting fact: I wrote chapters 1 and 2 of this book as a member of Capitol Hill Baptist Church. I write this last chapter as a member of a CHBC church plant—Cheverly Baptist Church.

WHAT IF THERE ARE NO OTHER GOOD CHURCHES TO SEND PEOPLE TO?

The absence of other healthy churches nearby makes partnerships and referrals difficult. But that's like saying there are no good schools nearby for one's children. It's a tough reality, but it doesn't change one's responsibility to educate one's children. It doesn't invalidate the rules. Likewise, a lack of good churches nearby doesn't change what a church is according to Jesus, or our responsibilities to it.

Therefore, a church in this situation needs either to build or rent a bigger building or to work harder at planting other churches. If the Lord is truly blessing a church with real Spirit-given growth and not just the apparent growth of so many attractional churches, he's probably also raising up pastors within that congregation. So pray! Pray that God would provide a bigger building or more pastors with whom to plant. Do you think the Almighty will be reluctant to give such gifts (see Matt. 7:9–11)?

I could write the section on referral and partnership because I lived through it at CHBC. And I could leave CHBC, though my affections for its pastors and members root deep, because CHBC helped inculcate these catholic sensibilities.

I first arrived at CHBC in 1996 when around 150 people attended. I then watched the building fill up over a number of years and then hit a ceiling at about a thousand members around 2012.

I sat on the elder board as we neared and then reached capacity. We had a number of long conversations about what to do. We even took whole-day retreats. Building a bigger building was (is) impossible because of the building's landlocked location. What became clear after half a dozen conversations was that, apart from a second service or site, there would be no magic pill to fix our full building. CHBC was and would remain stuck at its present size. And so it has been since around 2012.

Through these years, however, CHBC began to plant new churches or assist in the revitalization of old ones in the DC metropolitan area:

- First, CHBC sent Mike McKinley and half a dozen members to the Virginia suburbs to revitalize Guilford Baptist Church, which then merged with Sterling Park Baptist. The new Sterling Park has since planted several churches of its own, including a Spanish-speaking church.
- A couple of years later two dozen members left CHBC with Mike Law to revitalize, then plant, then revitalize (it's a long story!) Arlington Baptist Church.
- Garrett Conner departed with a dozen folk to pastor La Plata Baptist Church.
- After several failed attempts, CHBC sent several elders, including Garrett Kell as lead pastor, and several dozen members to Del Ray Baptist Church. Del Ray had about ten in attendance then; now it has around four hundred members and it is spiritually thriving.

- Shortly thereafter, Nick Roark left with a dozen people to revitalize Franconia Baptist Church.
- About the same time, Thabiti Anyabwile took several elders and almost seventy members to plant Anacostia River Church.
- My own Cheverly Baptist Church left CHBC with me, two other non-staff elders, staff pastor John Joseph, and over sixty members. We are now one year old.
- Beyond all this, CHBC has sent pastors to churches in this area and around the world, such as Zach Schlegel at First Baptist Upper Marlboro.
- CHBC has also adopted various plants and planters who didn't come from us but wanted to plant in DC. Nathan Knight, for instance, made himself a constant presence in our lives and meetings while planting Restoration Church in Northwest DC, until the point came that we couldn't help but trust him and send members with him.

CHBC has prioritized revitalizations over plants. Revitalizations, like plants, raise up new and vibrant witnesses for the gospel. But they have additional benefits: they clean up a poor witness, gain a church building, and provide ministry and care for the few old saints left in the dying church. They're a two for one: clean up the old and sponsor the new. Yet revitalizations depend upon a dying church's request for help, which doesn't happen every day. So they can be harder to come by. As such, CHBC has sought to be ready for both plants and revitalization projects.

My own church was a plant because no gospel-preaching church existed in the suburb of Cheverly, where around a hundred CHBC members lived. Let me tell you just one story about how it began, because Mark Dever's posture throughout—I believe—wonderfully conveys the humble, catholic attitude we all need. Mark, believe it or not, never liked the idea of a Cheverly church plant because of its proximity to CHBC. And he had quietly made this argument to the elders for years. But then, one Sunday evening in 2017, four of us non-staff elders sat down with Mark and told him we wanted to plant in Cheverly. After he heard our pitch, the first words out of this talented pastor's mouth were "Brothers, this is not what I would have chosen, but since I have four elders all saying this to me, I assume it must be from the Lord. I will support it entirely." And he did—in public and private. He could have said we would work better together than apart. He could have recommended an institutional connection. He could have whispered his misgivings to other elders, undermining the project. Instead, he encouraged us and got behind us, even to the budgetary hurt of CHBC, which continues as of this writing.

None of these plants or revitalizations have emptied a significant percentage of chairs at CHBC, but they do help to create space for new members to join on a constant cycle. No one attempting to join CHBC has been rebuffed, nor do I expect anyone will be. The building and parking lot remain packed on Sunday mornings. It remains inconvenient, and those who don't return are probably the most complacent and the least committed. One might argue that these are the very ones who most need the church. Or one might argue that people like these will benefit most from the relational dynamics of a smaller church, and leaving CHBC will help them find one.

Ultimately, the process of planting and revitalizing, combined with the natural process of people moving into and out of DC, relieves enough pressure to always keep the doors open to newcomers, even if it doesn't remove all the inconveniences. A plant or revitalization effort might take only one or two dozen people at the outset, but dozens more will trickle out over the years. People see that their friends who went with the first batch are flourishing, and then they follow. And many new arrivals to that neighborhood will join the new church nearby rather than drive thirty minutes to the church with the famous preacher.

Yet here is what's crucial: the inconveniences and pressures of a full building force—and I do mean force—the church as a whole to adopt a catholic posture. First, we recognize our need to plant and to revitalize. Second, close friends leave and join those churches, which creates an interest in their success and health. These separate churches then delight to hear of one another's success and growth, and pray for one another regularly. Each church is fully autonomous, enjoying all the natural and biblical benefits of being one site and one service. Yet there is no turf war or competition between us. Instead, the ongoing partnership among elders and members alike remains automatic, aided by frequent meals, conferences, and even an annual retreat among the different lead pastors.

Just this last Sunday, Garrett Kell, who pastors one of CHBC's revitalization projects, preached in our church, Cheverly Baptist. After the sermon, our lead pastor, John, interviewed him for ten minutes. Then we all prayed for him and his church.

Insofar as the unique relationship between mother and daughter churches trains all of us to adopt a more catholic posture, that posture then more easily applies to our bearing toward churches with whom we do not share our history. CHBC, for instance, has partnered with a Presbyterian and an Anglican church to host lunchtime evangelism talks downtown. Arlington Baptist recently joined with a Presbyterian church to host a lecture on the Reformation. And so on.

From time to time I hear megachurch pastors explain, "You can't plant fast enough to solve your growth problems." I agree. But moving to a second service or site removes a good pressure on the church to look outward, to work harder at planting, to work harder at raising up more leaders, to work harder at partnering with other churches, to work harder at trusting other churches and God's work in them. Catholicity is grounded in trust—trust in God and trust in other churches. Second services and sites are like pressure-release valves that let us avoid that need for trust, catholicity, and partnership. Yet that pressure is good for a pastor's soul and the soul of his church because it reminds us of our finitude.

No, we cannot save the city by ourselves. Yes, we must trust God in places where we would prefer control. Yes, we will have to spend more time investing in other ministries. No, no one on this earth will give us credit or glory when that separate church grows and prospers. Yes, eventually, one day, maybe, we will be able to look across the landscape of a city and see dozens of healthy churches, all praise going to God. The gold-medalist pastor didn't build a megachurch, but now there's a team with dozens of gold, silver, and bronze medalists. Go, Team Kingdom!

Peaceable Divisions

The last alternative to multiple services and sites involves what Baptists in the nineteenth century called "amicable separations" or "voluntary divides" or "peaceable divisions." A peaceable division is just that: a church peaceably dividing in two, by agreement, for the purposes of multiplying churches and carrying out the Great Commission. Throughout the United States, Baptist churches would sometimes divide in two, and then again, and then again, until four or five churches existed.[4]

For instance, the First Baptist church of Lowell, Massachusetts, began the Second Baptist church by sending out seventy of its members in September 1831. Likewise, the First Baptist church in Albany, New York, established a second church at Pearl Street by sending 122 members, along with the senior pastor of the first church. The church at Oliver Street in New York sent out "very many" of its members both to start a second church and to revitalize several other dying churches. A first church in Boston constituted a second, which then constituted four more in the ensuing years.

Yet this practice is not limited to the nineteenth century. In early 2012, the elders at Bardstown Christian Fellowship in Bardstown, Kentucky, recognized they would soon outgrow their meeting space. So they presented the congregation with a plan called, "On-site Church Planting." The congregation accepted it. In August of that year, the church divided in two. Yet both kept meeting

WHAT IF HUNDREDS OF NON-CHRISTIANS SUDDENLY SHOW UP?

Go back and read the box entitled "Transitions and Other Irregularities" (p. 110) where I recommended allowing for occasional irregularities in matters of church polity. I agree a church should do what it reasonably can to accommodate any non-Christian—or several hundred of them—who show up on any given Sunday. On September 16, 2001, the first Sunday after both buildings of the World Trade Center collapsed, Redeemer Presbyterian Church in New York City, then pastored by Tim Keller, ballooned from an ordinary attendance of 2800 to 5400 people. The pastors and staff scrambled and then announced an additional service for later that day.* That strikes me as the right decision, just as cutting a hole in the roof and lowering a paraplegic to hear Jesus—I think we can assume—was a pretty good decision.

As I said in that earlier box, the New Testament makes allowances for churches to do irregular things in order to accommodate the contingencies of the moment. Yet there's a difference between short-term accommodations and permanent structures. Short-term accommodations don't redefine what a church is. A refugee might be happy to live in a tent for a week, less happy to do so for a decade. Certainly, we shouldn't cut holes in our roofs every week. Redeemer's impromptu service effectively created an evangelistic event, not a sudden and permanent growth of the church.

* John Starke, "New York's Post-9/11 Church Boom," The Gospel Coalition, September 7, 2011, https://www.thegospelcoalition.org/article/new-yorks-post-911 -church-boom.

in the same building. It was a church plant in their own building. The new church, Grace Fellowship Church, meets at 8:30 a.m. The original church, renamed Redeemer Fellowship Church, meets at 11:00 a.m. To facilitate property sharing, they established BCF Network, which owns the property and its furnishings and allows the two churches to share everything in common. Plus, they jointly fund a church administrator and share all facility expenses. They are two churches in one location.[5]

Meanwhile, on the other side of the planet, Colin Clark led his three-year-old church in East Asia to divide peaceably. They too were reaching building capacity. Looking at a city map, they noticed that, while the church met in the northeast quadrant, almost half came from the southwest. So the eighty-four members sent thirty-nine off to establish a church in the southwest, along with more than half the giving.

Planting by peaceable division is the most radical and self-denying alternative. It also paints a wonderful picture of Christian sacrifice, love, and generosity. Writing about his church's experience, Clark observes, "Church planting by peaceable division was really, really hard, but also really, really worth it." The biggest struggles, he continues,

> involved emotional difficulties: friendships complicated, healthy community shaken up. On top of that came the difficulties of not having enough elders, deacons, and money. Our church was left with less experienced preachers; we also lost a majority of the large families. I could go on because the list of challenges isn't short.

For all the burdens, he says they experienced "far more blessings."

> Our church in the northeast has had more room for more people to come in and hear God's Word proclaimed, and the plant in the southwest has been able to provide a healthy church for many who hadn't heard of our church or who had but didn't

want to make the hour-plus trek across the city. We've also been able to start an association that seeks to strengthen even more local churches.

He continues:

On a personal level, the whole experience of church planting strengthened my faith. I had to trust God like never before and take my hands off situations that, in my flesh, I so greatly wanted to manipulate. God met me—and all of us—in the midst of any confusion, and truly gave us peace that surpasses understanding.[6]

Transitioning to One Assembly

If your church already has more than one service or site, how do you transition back to one assembly? A hundred different sets of circumstances will require a hundred different pathways. My short counsel for any situation is to do it slowly and responsibly. If you are the pastor of two or three services, or two or three sites, you are the pastor of two or three churches. You will give an account for all of them (Heb. 13:17). Therefore, you want to see to it that all of them are cared for well as you peaceably divide.

First, make sure each church (service or site) is left with a godly man or men who meet the qualifications Paul gave to Titus and Timothy for elders. By this token one of the most critical steps in a transition is raising up more leaders.

Second, very often a host of financial commitments complicates any plans to disentangle churches. This is a good reason to move slowly so that such commitments might be handled responsibly.

Third, be open to creative solutions. Bardstown Christian Fellowship's decision to plant a second church in the same building is just such a creative solution. It might not work in the long run, but it helps the church transition.

Fourth, teaching the congregation(s) step-by-step through this transition is critical. They deserve to learn both why you would reverse course and what kind of timetable you have in mind. You might even involve them in deciding upon a transition timetable, whether slow, medium, or fast. Certainly, every step must be taken only after much prayer.

For my part, I would not accept a pastorate in a multisite or multiservice church from the get-go, unless that church recognized and accepted my intentions to help them peaceably divide. By the same token, I would probably resign from a church that refused to divide, but I would willingly take several years to transition if they were willing to take that route.

Wanted: Catholic Pastors

I hope that a number of readers will find the biblical and etymological discussions in the previous chapters interesting, even compelling. Maybe that's you. Maybe you now concede that, yes, the word *ekklēsia* means "assembly" and, what's more, it's pretty hard to find multisite churches in the New Testament text. Maybe you will even admit that the one-assembly church (a redundant phrase) is pastorally ideal. Still, you wonder, is adopting such a commitment realistic in this day and age? Aren't we too far down this path? And since the Bible doesn't explicitly forbid it, maybe it's okay.

First, I'd remind you that the Bible's design for churches will prove best for strengthening Christians and reaching non-Christians. Compromising that might gain you something in the short term, but you'll lose it in the long term. You don't want to fight Jesus.

Second, I'd remind you of your job description, if you're a pastor. The vision of this book will not likely take hold unless you grasp your responsibility to invest in pastors and churches beyond the four walls of your own church. I don't want you to build the structures of a bishopric (indeed, an argument against multiple sites is an argument against precisely that). But I want you to adopt the mentality of a bishop—someone devoted to the good and growth of the churches and pastors in your region. I want you to be a catholic pastor.

Along these lines, I'll conclude with the words of Mark Dever:

I love being a pastor and I love pastors. I thank God for pastors and try to work to serve them as he gives me opportunity.

Perhaps it's because of this very love that sometimes I also find myself saddened by pastors. How many times have pastors made remarks that seem to show that their dreams and hopes begin and end at the doors of their own church? While there is sometimes admirable contentment and humility in this, I fear that other times it is self-absorption and small-mindedness.

Some pastors' hopes seem to be otherwise distorted—like pastors who root for their denominations like fans do for their sports teams! I remember one pastor telling me with excitement what percentage of people in his state were members of his denomination, trends of growth, and an array of other denominational statistics. When I asked him about percentages of people in his state who claimed to be evangelical Christians—that is, they claim to believe the same gospel we do—he had no idea. He seemed not to have thought of the question before.

Brother pastors, how is it that we can be more concerned about who is in our denomination than about who is in Christ's kingdom? Do we think more in terms of swelling the number of those in our congregation, or of those in the church of God, whichever local congregation they may be a member of?

I long for God to raise up more pastors who care more about conversions than the numerical growth of their own congregations.

I long for God to raise up more pastors who will work to develop a culture of care for and cooperation with other churches.

I long for God to raise up pastors who pray for revival for years, and who are *not* disappointed when God answers their prayers at another local church.[7]

Appendix 1

NEW TESTAMENT USES OF
EKKLĒSIA/"ASSEMBLY"

Here is a list of every occurrence of *ekklēsia* in the New Testament. I have used the ESV translation, but I've substituted the word *ekklēsia*/"assembly" or *ekklēsiai*/"assemblies" (regardless of case endings) for the word "church" or "churches" for reasons explained in the introduction (see "'Church' Not a Direct Translation of *Ekklēsia*," p. 20).

Usage Category 1: *Ekklēsia*/"Assembly" as "Gathering of Members"

In the following verses, the word *ekklēsia*/"assembly" appears to be used with a view to the actual assembly or gathering. That might be evident in each verse itself (e.g., 1 Cor. 11:18) or from its larger context (e.g., 1 Cor. 11:16). Therefore, I have inserted the *interpretive* phrase "gathering of members" in brackets to suggest that one could read the word *ekklēsia* or "assembly" that way.

Matthew 18:17. "If he refuses to listen to them, tell it to the *ekklēsia*/assembly [gathering of members]. And if he refuses to listen even to the *ekklēsia*/assembly [gathering of members], let him be to you as a Gentile and a tax collector."

Acts 11:22. "The report of this came to the ears of the *ekklēsia*/assembly [gathering of members] in Jerusalem, and they sent Barnabas to Antioch."

Acts 11:26. "For a whole year they met with the *ekklēsia*/assembly [gathering of members] and taught a great many people."

Acts 14:23. "And when they had appointed elders for them in every *ekklēsia*/assembly [gathering of members], with prayer and fasting they committed them to the Lord in whom they had believed."

Acts 15:3. "So, being sent on their way by the *ekklēsia*/assembly [gathering of members], they passed through both Phoenicia and Samaria, describing in detail the conversion of the Gentiles, and brought great joy to all the brothers."

Acts 15:4. "When they came to Jerusalem, they were welcomed by the *ekklēsia*/assembly [gathering of members] and the apostles and the elders, and they declared all that God had done with them."

Acts 15:22. "Then it seemed good to the apostles and the elders, with the whole *ekklēsia*/assembly [gathering of members], to choose men from among them and send them to Antioch with Paul and Barnabas."

Acts 18:22. "When he had landed at Caesarea, he went up and greeted the *ekklēsia*/assembly [gathering of members], and then went down to Antioch."

Romans 16:5. "Greet also the *ekklēsia*/assembly [gathering of members] in their house."

Romans 16:23. "Gaius, who is host to me and to the whole *ekklēsia*/assembly [gathering of members], greets you."

1 Corinthians 4:17. "That is why I sent you Timothy, my beloved and faithful child in the Lord, to remind you of my ways in Christ, as I teach them everywhere in every *ekklēsia*/assembly [gathering of members]."

1 Corinthians 6:4. "So if you have such cases, why do you lay them before those who have no standing in the *ekklēsia*/assembly [gathering of members]?"

1 Corinthians 11:16. "If anyone is inclined to be contentious, we have no such practice, nor do the *ekklēsiai*/assemblies of God [gatherings of members (with emphasis on God's ownership of them)]."

1 Corinthians 11:18. "For, in the first place, when you come together as a *ekklēsia*/assembly [gathering of members], I hear that there are divisions among you."

1 Corinthians 11:22. "What! Do you not have houses to eat and drink in? Or do you despise the *ekklēsia*/assembly of God [gathering of members (with emphasis on God's ownership of them)] and humiliate those who have nothing?"

1 Corinthians 14:4. "The one who speaks in a tongue builds up himself, but the one who prophesies builds up the *ekklēsia*/assembly [gathering of members]."

1 Corinthians 14:5. "Now I want you all to speak in tongues, but even more to prophesy. The one who prophesies is greater than the one who speaks in tongues, unless someone interprets, so that the *ekklēsia*/assembly [gathering of members] may be built up."

1 Corinthians 14:12. "So with yourselves, since you are eager for manifestations of the Spirit, strive to excel in building up the *ekklēsia*/assembly [gathering of members]."

1 Corinthians 14:19. "Nevertheless, in *ekklēsia*/assembly [the gathering of members] I would rather speak five words with my mind in order to instruct others, than ten thousand words in a tongue."

1 Corinthians 14:23. "If, therefore, the whole *ekklēsia*/assembly [gathering of members] comes together and all speak in tongues, and outsiders or unbelievers enter, will they not say that you are out of your minds?"

1 Corinthians 14:28. "But if there is no one to interpret, let each of them keep silent in *ekklēsia*/assembly [the gathering of members] and speak to himself and to God."

1 Corinthians 14:33–35. "As in all the *ekklēsiai*/assemblies [gatherings of members] of the saints, the women should keep silent in the *ekklēsiai*/assemblies [gatherings of members]. . . . If there is anything they desire to learn, let them ask their husbands at home. For it is shameful for a woman to speak in *ekklēsia*/assembly [the gathering of members]."

1 Corinthians 16:1. "Now concerning the collection for the saints: as I directed the *ekklēsiai*/assemblies [gatherings of members] of Galatia, so you also are to do."

1 Corinthians 16:19b. "Aquila and Prisca, together with the *ekklēsia*/assembly [gathering of members] in their house, send you hearty greetings in the Lord."

2 Corinthians 8:19. "And not only that, but he has been appointed by the *ekklēsiai*/assemblies [gatherings of members] to travel with us as we carry out this act of grace that is being ministered by us."

2 Corinthians 8:24. "So give proof before the *ekklēsiai*/assemblies [gatherings of members] of your love and of our boasting about you to these men."

Colossians 4:15. "Give my greetings to the brothers at Laodicea, and to Nympha and the *ekklēsia*/assembly [gathering of members] in her house."

Colossians 4:16. "And when this letter has been read among you, have it also read in the *ekklēsia*/assembly [gathering of members] of the Laodiceans; and see that you also read the letter from Laodicea."

Philemon 2. "... and Apphia our sister and Archippus our fellow soldier, and the *ekklēsia*/assembly [gathering of members] in your house..."

3 John 6. "... who testified to your love before the *ekklēsia*/assembly [gathering of members]. You will do well to send them on their journey in a manner worthy of God."

3 John 9. "I have written something to the *ekklēsia*/assembly [gathering of members], but Diotrephes, who likes to put himself first, does not acknowledge our authority."

Usage Category 2: *Ekklēsia*/"Assembly" as "Members"/"Membership"

In the following verses, the word *ekklēsia* appears to be used *without* a view to the act of assembling or gathering. The focus is on the people—their identity as a marked-off group—like referring to a "team" outside the context of the game (e.g., "The team spent the evening in separate rooms at the Hilton"). For instance, when someone who is sick calls for "the elders of the *ekklēsia*/assembly" (James 5:14), I don't assume the sick person is calling them away from the assembly. The word *ekklēsia* is being used as an identifier of a people who are made a church by their assembling (as I've argued in this book).

Acts 8:1, 3. "And Saul approved of his execution. And there arose on that day a great persecution against the *ekklēsia*/assembly [members/membership] in Jerusalem, and they were all scattered throughout the regions of Judea and Samaria, except the apostles.... But Saul was ravaging the *ekklēsia*/assembly [members/

membership], and entering house after house, he dragged off men and women and committed them to prison."

Acts 9:31. "So the *ekklēsia*/assembly [membership] throughout all Judea and Galilee and Samaria had peace and was being built up. And walking in the fear of the Lord and in the comfort of the Holy Spirit, it multiplied."

Acts 12:1. "About that time Herod the king laid violent hands on some who belonged to the *ekklēsia*/assembly [membership]."

Acts 14:27. "And when they arrived and gathered the *ekklēsia*/assembly [members/membership] together, they declared all that God had done with them, and how he had opened a door of faith to the Gentiles."

Acts 20:17. "Now from Miletus he sent to Ephesus and called the elders of the *ekklēsia*/assembly [membership] to come to him."

Acts 20:28. "Pay careful attention to yourselves and to all the flock, in which the Holy Spirit has made you overseers, to care for the *ekklēsia*/assembly [members/membership] of God, which he obtained with his own blood."

Romans 16:1. "I commend to you our sister Phoebe, a servant of the *ekklēsia*/assembly [members/membership] at Cenchreae."

Romans 16:4. ". . . who risked their necks for my life, to whom not only I give thanks but all the *ekklēsiai*/assemblies [members/memberships] of the Gentiles give thanks as well."

1 Corinthians 5:12. "For what have I to do with judging outsiders? Is it not those inside the *ekklēsia*/assembly [membership] whom you are to judge?"

1 Corinthians 10:32. "Give no offense to Jews or to Greeks or to the *ekklēsia*/assembly [members/membership] of God."

1 Corinthians 15:9. "For I am the least of the apostles, unworthy to be called an apostle, because I persecuted the *ekklēsia*/assembly [members/membership] of God."

2 Corinthians 8:1. "We want you to know, brothers, about the grace of God that has been given among the *ekklēsiai*/assemblies [memberships] of Macedonia."

2 Corinthians 11:8. "I robbed other *ekklēsiai*/assemblies [memberships] by accepting support from them in order to serve you."

2 Corinthians 11:28. "And, apart from other things, there is the daily pressure on me of my anxiety for all the *ekklēsiai*/assemblies [memberships]."

2 Corinthians 12:13. "For in what were you less favored than the rest of the *ekklēsiai*/assemblies [memberships], except that I myself did not burden you?"

Galatians 1:13. "For you have heard of my former life in Judaism, how I persecuted the *ekklēsia*/assembly [membership (of Jerusalem)] of God violently and tried to destroy it."

Galatians 1:22. "And I was still unknown in person to the *ekklēsiai*/assemblies [memberships] of Judea that are in Christ."

Philippians 3:6. ". . . as to zeal, a persecutor of the *ekklēsia*/assembly [membership (of Jerusalem)]; as to righteousness under the law, blameless."

Philippians 4:15. "And you Philippians yourselves know that in the beginning of the gospel, when I left Macedonia, no *ekklēsia*/assembly [membership] entered into partnership with me in giving and receiving, except you only."

1 Thessalonians 2:14. "For you, brothers, became imitators of the *ekklēsiai*/assemblies [memberships] of God in Christ Jesus that are in Judea."

1 Timothy 3:5. "For if someone does not know how to manage his own household, how will he care for God's *ekklēsia*/assembly [members/membership]?"

1 Timothy 3:15. "If I delay, you may know how one ought to behave in the household of God, which is the *ekklēsia*/assembly [membership] of the living God, a pillar and buttress of the truth.

1 Timothy 5:16. If any believing woman has relatives who are widows, let her care for them. Let the *ekklēsia*/assembly [membership] not be burdened, so that it may care for those who are truly widows."

James 5:14. "Is anyone among you sick? Let him call for the elders of the *ekklēsia*/assembly [membership], and let them pray over him, anointing him with oil in the name of the Lord."

Revelation 1:20. "As for the mystery of the seven stars that you saw in my right hand, and the seven golden lampstands, the seven stars are the angels of the seven *ekklēsiai*/assemblies [memberships], and the seven lampstands are the seven *ekklēsiai*/assemblies [memberships]."

Revelation 2:23. ". . . and I will strike her children dead. And all the *ekklēsiai*/assemblies [memberships] will know that I am he who searches mind and heart, and I will give to each of you according to your works."

Usage Category 3: *Ekklēsia*/"Assembly" Either as "Gathering of Members" or as "Members/Membership"

The following verses, in my judgment, could be interpreted as belonging to either of the categories above. For instance, I assume that Paul wrote "To the *ekklēsiai*/assemblies of Galatia" with a view to those letters being read to the gathered *ekklēsiai*/"assemblies" of Galatia. Still, one could reasonably read this without a view to the gathered assembly but simply with the people who assemble in mind. For a few of the verses below, I'm simply unsure of which of these two categories the usage falls into (e.g., Acts 5:11). So, rather than forcing a judgment, this category might simply be relabeled "I'm not sure."

Acts 5:11–12. "And great fear came upon the whole *ekklēsia*/assembly [gathering of members *or* membership] and upon all who heard of these things. Now many signs and wonders were regularly done among the people by the hands of the apostles. And they were all together in Solomon's Portico."

Acts 12:5. "So Peter was kept in prison, but earnest prayer for him was made to God by the *ekklēsia*/assembly [gathering of members *or* members/membership]." (But see v. 12.)

Acts 13:1–3. "Now there were in the *ekklēsia*/assembly [gathering of members *or* membership] at Antioch prophets and teachers, Barnabas . . . and Saul. While they were worshiping the Lord and fasting, the Holy Spirit said, 'Set apart for me Barnabas and Saul. . . .' Then after fasting and praying they laid their hands on them and sent them off."

Acts 15:41. "And he went through Syria and Cilicia, strengthening the *ekklēsiai*/assemblies [gatherings of members *or* memberships]."

Acts 16:4–5. "As they went on their way through the cities, they delivered to them for observance the decisions that had been reached by the apostles and elders who were in Jerusalem. So the *ekklēsiai*/ assemblies [gatherings of members *or* memberships] were strengthened in the faith, and they increased in numbers daily."

Romans 16:16. "Greet one another with a holy kiss. All the *ekklēsiai*/ assemblies [gatherings of members *or* memberships] of Christ greet you."

1 Corinthians 1:2. "To the *ekklēsia*/assembly [gathering of members *or* members/membership] of God that is in Corinth, to those sanctified in Christ Jesus, called to be saints together with all those who in every place call upon the name of our Lord Jesus Christ..."

1 Corinthians 7:17. "Only let each person lead the life that the Lord has assigned to him, and to which God has called him. This is my rule in all the *ekklēsiai*/assemblies [gatherings of members *or* memberships]."

1 Corinthians 16:19. "The *ekklēsiai*/assemblies [gatherings of members *or* memberships] of Asia send you greetings."

2 Corinthians 1:1. "Paul, an apostle of Christ Jesus by the will of God, and Timothy our brother, To the *ekklēsia*/assembly [gathering of members *or* members/membership] of God that is at Corinth, with all the saints who are in the whole of Achaia..."

2 Corinthians 8:18. "With him we are sending the brother who is famous among all the *ekklēsiai*/assemblies [gatherings of members *or* memberships] for his preaching of the gospel."

2 Corinthians 8:23. "As for Titus, he is my partner and fellow worker for your benefit. And as for our brothers, they are messengers of the *ekklēsiai*/assemblies [gatherings of members *or* memberships], the glory of Christ."

Galatians 1:2. "...and all the brothers who are with me, To the *ekklēsiai*/assemblies [gatherings of members *or* memberships] of Galatia."

1 Thessalonians 1:1. "Paul, Silvanus, and Timothy, To the *ekklēsia*/assembly [gathering of members *or* membership] of the Thessalonians in God the Father and the Lord Jesus Christ..."

2 Thessalonians 1:1. "Paul, Silvanus, and Timothy, To the *ekklēsia*/assembly [gathering of members *or* membership] of the Thessalonians in God our Father and the Lord Jesus Christ..."

2 Thessalonians 1:4. "Therefore we ourselves boast about you in the *ekklēsiai*/assemblies [gatherings of members *or* memberships] of God for your steadfastness and faith in all your persecutions and in the afflictions that you are enduring."

3 John 10. "So if I come, I will bring up what he is doing, talking wicked nonsense against us. And not content with that, he refuses to welcome the brothers, and also stops those who want to and puts them out of the *ekklēsia*/assembly [gathering of members *or* membership]."

Revelation 1:4. "John to the seven *ekklēsiai*/assemblies [gatherings of members *or* memberships] that are in Asia . . ."

Revelation 1:11. "Write what you see in a book and send it to the seven *ekklēsiai*/assemblies [gatherings of members *or* memberships], to Ephesus and to Smyrna and to Pergamum and to Thyatira and to Sardis and to Philadelphia and to Laodicea."

Revelation 2:1. "To the angel of the *ekklēsia*/assembly [gathering of members *or* membership] in Ephesus write . . ."

Revelation 2:7. "He who has an ear, let him hear what the Spirit says to the *ekklēsiai*/assemblies [gatherings of members *or* memberships]."

The same pattern as the *ekklēsia*/"assembly" of Ephesus holds for the six subsequent *ekklēsiai*/"assemblies" mentioned in Revelation 2:8, 11, 12, 17, 18, 29; 3:1, 6, 7, 13, 14, 22.

Revelation 22:16. "I, Jesus, have sent my angel to testify to you about these things for the *ekklēsiai*/assemblies [gatherings of members *or* memberships]."

Usage Category 4: *Ekklēsia*/"Assembly" as the Universal Church

The following verses refer to the universal church, which I understand to be a heavenly and/or eschatological assembly. This is most explicit in the Hebrews text. Yet it's a property of an already–not yet eschatology in all these texts.

Matthew 16:18. "And I tell you, you are Peter, and on this rock I will build my *ekklēsia*/assembly [assembly of restored Israel] and the gates of hell shall not prevail against it."

1 Corinthians 12:28. "And God has appointed in the *ekklēsia*/assembly [heavenly or eschatological assembly] first apostles, second prophets, third teachers, then miracles, then gifts of healing, helping, administrating, and various kinds of tongues."

Ephesians 1:22. "And he put all things under his feet and gave him as head over all things to the *ekklēsia*/assembly [heavenly or eschatological assembly]."

Ephesians 3:10. ". . . so that through the *ekklēsia*/assembly [heavenly or eschatological assembly] the manifold wisdom of God might now be made known to the rulers and authorities in the heavenly places."

Ephesians 3:21. "To him be glory in the *ekklēsia*/assembly [heavenly or eschatological assembly] and in Christ Jesus throughout all generations, forever and ever. Amen."

Ephesians 5:23–25, 27, 29, 32. "For the husband is the head of the wife even as Christ is the head of the *ekklēsia*/assembly [heavenly or eschatological assembly], his body, and is himself its Savior. Now as the *ekklēsia*/assembly submits to Christ, so also wives should submit in everything to their husbands. Husbands, love your wives, as Christ loved the *ekklēsia*/assembly and gave himself up for her . . . so that he might present the *ekklēsia*/assembly to himself in splendor, without spot or wrinkle or any such thing, that she might be holy and without blemish. . . . For no one ever hated his own flesh, but nourishes and cherishes it, just as Christ does the *ekklēsia*/assembly. . . . This mystery is profound, and I am saying that it refers to Christ and the *ekklēsia*/assembly."

Colossians 1:18. "And he is the head of the body, the *ekklēsia*/assembly [heavenly or eschatological assembly]. He is the beginning, the firstborn from the dead, that in everything he might be preeminent."

Colossians 1:24. "Now I rejoice in my sufferings for your sake, and in my flesh I am filling up what is lacking in Christ's afflictions for the sake of his body, that is, the *ekklēsia*/assembly [heavenly or eschatological assembly]."

Hebrews 12:22–24. "But you have come to Mount Zion and to the city of the living God, the heavenly Jerusalem, and to innumerable angels in festal gathering, and to the *ekklēsia*/assembly [heavenly or eschatological assembly] of the firstborn who are enrolled in heaven, and to God, the judge of all, and to the spirits of the righteous made perfect, and to Jesus, the mediator of a new covenant."

Usage Category 5: *Ekklēsia*/**"Assembly" as "Gathering"**

Acts 19:32. "Now some cried out one thing, some another, for the *ekklēsia*/assembly [gathering] was in confusion, and most of them did not know why they had come together."

Acts 19:39. "But if you seek anything further, it shall be settled in the regular *ekklēsia*/assembly [gathering]."

Acts 19:41. "And when he had said these things, he dismissed the *ekklēsia*/assembly [gathering]."

Appendix 2

DOES ACTS 9:31 REFER TO A REGIONAL "CHURCH"?

Anne Rabe[1]

Acts 9:31 presents a unique challenge to the premise of this book, for there we find Luke applying the singular ἐκκλησία to *three* demarcated geographical regions (Judea, Galilee, and Samaria). As such, it seems at first glance to indicate neither the universal church nor a specific local gathering, but rather a multiregional—or multisite, for our purposes—body.[2] Does this instance then undermine the "one assembly" argument set forth in the preceding pages? In short, no, for Luke's singular ἐκκλησία in Acts 9:31 should actually be read as the plural "churches." To see how this works, though, we must do a little scholarly digging.

Let us begin with the verse itself and a brief overview of its interpretation. As Luke ends his narrative of Paul's conversion, he offers a summarizing statement: "So the church [ἐκκλησία] throughout all Judea and Galilee and Samaria had peace and was being built up. And walking in the fear of the Lord and in the comfort of the Holy Spirit, it multiplied" (Acts 9:31).[3]

Now, some scholars and commentators have in fact interpreted the singular ἐκκλησία here as designating the universal church, and a number have employed it in the service of multisite ecclesiology.[4] Many, though, have recently taken up the view that Luke, through this singular, is referring to a larger "church" community encompassing the three regions of Judea, Galilee, and Samaria.[5] Yet all of these interpretations are problematic. First, Luke's typical practice is to use ἐκκλησία in the singular to denote a local congregation— a discrete, single-site assembly.[6] Second, nowhere else in the New Testament is this singular applied in any universalizing sense to a delineated geographical region as apparently occurs here.[7] So how are we to reconcile this seeming dilemma?

To arrive at an answer, we must lean into the Greek of this verse and its textual transmission. I will argue that ἐκκλησία in Acts 9:31 should be understood as a plural for two reasons. First and foremost, the specific Greek word Luke uses to express "throughout" in this verse, the preposition κατά (followed by the genitive), amplifies and extends whatever governs it; and as a result, ἐκκλησία takes on the force of the plural ἐκκλησίαι. And, second, a number of manuscripts do in fact read the plural at Acts 9:31 instead of the singular, and thus we find that others have understood ἐκκλησίαι in the same way over the course of the New Testament's transmission.

The Function of Κατά

Since the preposition κατά provides the most crucial piece of evidence for this argument, I'll begin with it. As a reminder, in Acts 9:31 Luke speaks of "the church *throughout* all Judea and Galilee and Samaria," and it is specifically κατά that Luke chooses to use for this expression. Since we're going to be working with Greek a good deal here and in the pages that follow, I offer the Greek of this verse below for ease of reference, with the κατά phrase italicized:

Ἡ μὲν οὖν ἐκκλησία *καθ᾽ ὅλης τῆς Ἰουδαίας καὶ Γαλιλαίας καὶ Σαμαρείας* εἶχεν εἰρήνην οἰκοδομουμένη καὶ πορευομένη τῷ φόβῳ τοῦ κυρίου καὶ τῇ παρακλήσει τοῦ ἁγίου πνεύματος ἐπληθύνετο. (Acts 9:31)[8]

But of course the significance of κατά is not readily apparent from just this one instance. We need to search the New Testament for other examples of κατά plus the genitive used to express "throughout," and we find a total of four more, all of which come from the writings of Luke (Luke 4:14; 23:5; Acts 9:42; 10:37). These additional examples serve as parallels for Luke's use of κατά in Acts 9:31—especially since they all derive from Luke himself—and illuminate the significance of this preposition. So let's have a look at them.

1. In Acts 9:42, Luke states that Peter's miraculous raising of Tabitha from the dead "became known *throughout* [κατά] all of Joppa."[9]
2. Similarly, in Acts 10:37, as Peter witnesses to Cornelius and his friends about the person and work of Jesus Christ, Peter grounds his testimony in the widespread reports about Jesus with which Cornelius and company were familiar: "You all know of the report that happened *throughout* [κατά] all of Judea."[10]
3. In addition, we read in Luke 4:14 that Jesus, after his period of temptation, returned to Galilee, and that "talk about him spread *throughout* [κατά] all the surrounding region."[11]
4. Finally, in Luke 23:5, after Pilate announces that he has found no fault in Jesus, the Jews respond by insisting that "[Jesus] is stirring up the people with his teaching *throughout* [κατά] all of Judea."[12]

Now, these four instances are not necessarily parallel in their specific subject matter—the first three deal with some sort of knowledge, news, or report, while the fourth concerns Jesus's teaching. But all four involve some sort of verbal communication—speech acts, if you will—since teaching, reporting, talking, and sharing knowledge all entail writing or speaking. Moreover, in each of the four this speech act, whatever it is, is *extended* through a specified geographical region, and that extension (or spreading) is achieved by κατά plus the genitive. To understand the force κατά bears in each of these instances, we need to consider how they would read *without* this prepositional phrase. The four parallels, without their κατά phrases, would result in the following brief statements:

1. "[The raising of Tabitha] became known" (Acts 9:42).
2. "You all know of the report that happened [τὸ γενόμενον ῥῆμα]" (Acts 10:37).
3. "Talk [φήμη] about [Jesus] spread" (Luke 4:14).
4. "[Jesus] is stirring up the people with his teaching" (Luke 23:5).

The central questions here are whether and to what extent these speech acts require repetition in and of themselves. Namely, do all these speech acts, as presented without κατά phrases, *have* to happen more than once? Because if they don't, then we can ascribe the proliferation required in their spreading *throughout* a given region to the preposition κατά. Indeed, some speech acts are inherently "iterative" in that their meaning necessitates more than one repetition or iteration of the act. Rumor is a good example of this, for a rumor can't be a rumor unless it is *repeated*. If Johnny tells only his friend David that Sally stole the cookie from the cookie jar, that isn't a rumor. Johnny has to first tell David, and then whisper it to Susan in the hallway later, and David and Susan must themselves pass the news on further. Such repetition is what makes a rumor. Accordingly, instance 3 above, involving "talk" or "rumor" (φήμη) about Jesus, is indeed inherently iterative. This "talk" or "rumor" must necessarily happen more than once simply *to be* "talk" or "rumor." It may happen with even greater frequency when the prepositional phrase is added, but κατά does not *make* it iterative.

But the same is not true of the others. They *could* entail repetition as presented above, without κατά, but they do not *have* to. Something can become known by a single act of communication (instance 1), a report can be made once (instance 2), and teaching can occur only one time (instance 4). If we remove the κατά phrases from each of these three, nothing in the text indicates inherent repetition of these acts. So whether or not these other three instances of speech acts are iterative in and of themselves is unclear, but what *is* clear is that once κατά is added, they certainly *are* iterative. For the raising of Tabitha to have become known throughout all of Joppa (instance 1), the news had to have been passed on multiple times. For Jesus to have taught throughout all of Judea (instance 4), he must have taught multiple times. And for the report about Jesus to have happened throughout all of Judea (instance 2), it must have occurred multiple times.

To see even more clearly the iterative power of κατά at work in these parallels, let's compare this last instance (2 above, Acts 10:37) with Luke 3:2, as Luke uses the same noun and verb in both. In Luke 3:2, we read that in the time of the high priesthood of Annas and Caiaphas, the "word" (ῥῆμα) of the Lord "happened" (ἐγένετο) to John the son of Zechariah while he was in the desert.[13] Here Luke uses ἐγένετο instead of the participle γενόμενον found in Acts 10:37, but otherwise the vocabulary is the same: both verses employ ῥῆμα and a form of γίγνομαι. Now, according to the text, did John experience one divine revelation or a series of revelations? The answer has to be one; "word" (ῥῆμα) is singular, and Luke tells us it just "happened" to him (ἐγένετο), the aorist tense here neither ingressive (indicating the beginning of action) nor iterative but a simple glimpse of the revelation effected (and thus it is often translated "came").[14] The word of the Lord came to John (the Baptist) *one time*, if not in reality, then at least according to the grammar of this verse; nothing in the text indicates otherwise. In contrast, in Acts 10:37 the "report" or "word" about Jesus, since it happened *throughout* all of Judea, must have occurred *multiple* times—time after time.

All this may seem tedious, but it shows that the vocabulary of instance 2 at least (ῥῆμα and γίγνομαι) can be and is used by Luke to indicate a speech act that happens only once (i.e., in Luke 3:2). In Acts 10:37 itself, though, the speech act—expressed through the same vocabulary—is clearly iterative, and so it must be the κατά phrase that lends this force. And this is the key and the whole point of the exercise above: κατά followed by the genitive, when it means "throughout," amplifies and extends whatever governs it in an iterative fashion. Let me explain it another way—if whatever governs κατά is *not* inherently iterative, κατά makes it iterative, and if it *is*, κατά makes it even more so. In Judea, Jesus taught and taught and taught (Luke 23:5), and talk about him spread in report after report after report (Acts 10:37). The four parallels above all display this iterative force of κατά to varying degrees.

And now we can finally return to Acts 9:31.[15] If we apply the same understanding of κατά here, we find that ἐκκλησία, since it governs κατά, becomes iterative (it's surely not on its own).[16] Accordingly, "the church throughout all Judea and Galilee and Samaria" is not *one* instance of a church but an iteration of churches—church after church after church. The singular here does not refer to the universal church, nor does it designate the scattered remnants of the Jerusalem church as one ἐκκλησία. Rather, it speaks of individual assemblies in each of the three regions of Judea, Galilee, and Samaria.[17] It is printed as a singular but should be felt as a plural, roughly akin to the grammatical phenomenon known as a collective singular.[18] Yet this usage is distinct to Luke's own phraseology—note that all five instances of this use of κατά are confined to his writings.[19] In sum, then, the preposition κατά in Acts 9:31 extends the singular church (ἐκκλησία) into an iteration of churches, multiple ἐκκλησίαι. We feel this when we read the text, but in fact we see it too when we look at the manuscripts.

Acts 9:31 and the Manuscript Tradition

Throughout this discussion we have assumed the singular ἐκκλησία as the proper reading at Acts 9:31. This is indeed what is printed in most editions, yet the plural ἐκκλησίαι (accompanied by plural verbs and participles as well) exists as a variant reading in some manuscripts, and it even appears occasionally as the preferred reading in editions of the Greek New Testament.[20] Now, I am not arguing in favor of the plural reading; the singular has been defended well already, and in support of this I might point out that in all five instances of κατά examined above, what governs κατά appears in the singular.[21] Rather, I want to make a simple point here: the very existence of these plural variants confirms that we are not alone in our understanding of ἐκκλησία. Indeed, what they suggest is that, at some point in the text's transmission, the singular ἐκκλησία was felt so strongly as "churches" that one or more scribes hyper-corrected the manuscripts and changed singular to plural to reflect this force.[22] We should not adopt the plural ἐκκλησίαι, but we should account for it in our interpretation. The singular ἐκκλησία *feels* and *reads* like ἐκκλησίαι—to us and to the saints and scholars of ages past.

Conclusion

A proper understanding of Acts 9:31 boils down to this, then: the singular ἐκκλησία designates multiple churches because κατά followed by the genitive creates an iteration of whatever governs it.[23] This is a distinctly Lukan means of expression and can be rightly understood only in light of the other four instances of its usage. We feel this plural sense of ἐκκλησία, and the manuscripts reflect it. To quote one commentator on this verse, "Obviously [Luke] intended to speak of all the Christian congregations" that were dispersed from the original Jerusalem church and settled in the regions of Judea, Galilee, and Samaria.[24] But, instead of wrestling to reconcile otherwise marginal or unattested uses to this natural interpretation, we see that Luke simply chose to express this through his own phraseology. "The *churches* throughout all Judea and Galilee and Samaria," we should read. The singular ἐκκλησία may indeed represent a community, but it is no more than a community of independent *churches* within these regions.

NOTES

Introduction

1. J. D. Greear, "Multi-Site or 'One-Service-Only?' A Question of Evangelistic Faithfulness," J. D. Greear Ministries, October 22, 2014, https://jdgreear.com/blog/multi-site-an-evangelistically-effective-model/.
2. Except when transliterating the term in quoted texts, I will forgo case endings of *ekklēsia* and the plural *ekklēsiai* for simplicity's sake.
3. Mark Driscoll and Gerry Breshears, *Vintage Church: Timeless Truths and Timely Methods* (Wheaton, IL: Crossway, 2008), 244.
4. Brad House and Gregg Allison, *Multichurch: Exploring the Future of Multisite* (Grand Rapids, MI: Zondervan, 2017), 21.
5. See Thomas White and John Mark Yeats, *Franchising McChurch: Feeding Our Obsession with Easy Christianity* (Colorado Springs: Cook, 2009).
6. Ed Stetzer, "The Explosive Growth of U.S. Megachurches, Even While Many Say Their Day Is Done," *CT*, February 19, 2013, http://www.christianitytoday.com/edstetzer/2013/february/explosive-growth-of-us-megachurches-even-while-many-say.html.
7. Warren Bird, "Big News—Multisite Churches Now Number More Than 5,000," Leadership Network, January 9, 2019, https://leadnet.org/big-news-multisite-churches-more-than-5000/.
8. Dave Adamson, "Church as We Know It Is Over," Fox News, March 11, 2019, https://www.foxnews.com/opinion/churches-as-we-know-it-are-over-here-is-how-to-engage-the-faithful.
9. Driscoll and Breshears, *Vintage Church*, 252, 255.
10. Bob Johnson, "The Christian Life Is More Like a Bus Ride Than a Motorcycle Ride," 9Marks, February 4, 2019, https://www.9marks.org/article/the-christian-life-is-more-like-a-bus-ride-than-a-motorcycle-ride/.

Chapter 1: A Church Is the Geography of Christ's Kingdom

1. "For Paul the ἐκκλησία is constituted not only by the act of assembling together in order to disperse after the conclusion of assembly; it maintains this name also outside of the concrete assembly. Thus [1 Cor.] 14:23: 'If,

therefore, the whole *church* assembles. . . .' Assembly for worship is the center and at the same time the criterion for life in the church" ("ἐκκλησία," in *Exegetical Dictionary of the New Testament*, ed. H. R. Balz and G. Schneider, vol. 1 [Grand Rapids, MI: Eerdmans, 1990], 413).

2. Miroslav Volf captures this when he writes:

> The life of the church is not exhausted in the act of assembly. Even if the church is not assembled, it does live on as a church in the mutual service its members render to one another and in its common mission to the world. The church is not simply an act of assembling; rather it assembles at a specific place (see 1 Cor. 14:23). It is the *people* who in a specific way assemble at a specific place. In its most concentrated form however, the church does manifest itself concretely in the act of assembling for worship, and this is constitutive for its ecclesiality. (*After Our Likeness* [Grand Rapids, MI: Eerdmans, 1998], 137)

3. John Webster's description of the visible church is worth quoting at length:

> The "visible" church is the "phenomenal" church—the church which has form, shape and endurance as a human undertaking, and which is present in the history of the world as a social project. The church is visible in the sense that, as a genuine creaturely event and assembly, it does not occur in "no-space" and is not a purely eschatological polity or culture. It is what men and women do because of the gospel. The church is a human gathering; it engages in human activities (speech, washing, eating and drinking); it has customs, texts, orders, procedures and possessions, like any other visible social entity. But how does it do and have these things? It does . . . by virtue of the work of the Holy Spirit. Only through the Holy Spirit's empowerment is the church a human assembly; and therefore only through the same Spirit is the church visible. . . .
>
> . . . The church, therefore, is natural history only because it is spiritual history, history by the Spirit's grace. ("The Visible Attests the Invisible," in *The Community of the Word: Toward an Evangelical Ecclesiology*, ed. Mark Husbands and Daniel Treier [Downers Grove, IL: IVP Academic, 2005], 101–2)

4. "The Christian community, which as the individual congregation represents the whole body, is just as visible and corporeal as the individual man" (*Theological Dictionary of the New Testament*, ed. Gerhard Kittel and Gerhard Friedrich, trans. Geoffrey W. Bromiley, 10 vols. [Grand Rapids, MI: Eerdmans, 1964–1976], 2:534, hereafter, *TDNT*).

5. Mark Seifrid, *The Second Letter to the Corinthians*, The Pillar New Testament Commentary (Grand Rapids, MI: Eerdmans, 2014), 7; see also, Bernd Wannenwetsch, *Political Worship* (New York: Oxford University Press, 2004), 137–39.

6. Liddell and Scott's lexicon, which focuses on ancient Greek literature, defines *ekklēsia* as "an assembly of the citizens regularly summoned, the legislative assembly" (H. G. Liddell, *A Lexicon: Abridged from Liddell and Scott's Greek-English Lexicon* [Oak Harbor, WA: Logos Research Systems, 1996], 239).

7. M. I. Finley, *Politics in the Ancient World* (New York: Cambridge University Press, 1983), 71; P. J. Rhodes, "Elections and Voting: Greek," in *Oxford Classical Dictionary*, 4th ed., ed. Simon Hornblower, Antony Spawforth, and Esther Eidinow (Oxford: Oxford University Press, 1996), 496.

8. Aristotle, *Politics* 6.2.28, in *The Basic Works of Aristotle*, ed. Richard McKeon (New York: Random House, 1941), 1266.

9. Ralph J. Korner writes: "Inscriptional evidence confirms the continued political relevance of civic *ekklēsiai* into at least the 2nd century CE. The Asia Minor *polis* of Termessos is a clear case in point. Onno van Nijf notes that Termessos had a regular assembly (*ennomos ekklēsia*) which held up to 4,500 citizens" ("*Ekklēsia* as a Jewish Synagogue Term: A Response to Erich Gruen," *Journal of the Jesus Movement in Its Jewish Setting* 4 [2017]: 132).

10. Roy Bowen Ward writes, "In ordinary usage, *ekklesia* meant the assembly, and not the body of people involved. . . . The *demos* (people) assembled in an *ekklesia*, but when they acted, it was said to be the action of the *demos*, not the *ekklesia*" ("Ekklesia: A Word Study," *Restoration Quarterly* 2 [1958]: 165). Likewise, Mogens Herman Hansen writes: "It is always the *demos* that passes a decree or votes by a show of hands, never the *ekklesia*. I conclude that *ekklesia* signifies a meeting of the assembly or the place where it meets, but the assembly itself was not the *ekklesia*, it was the *demos*" ("The Concepts of *Demos, Ekklesia*, and *Dikasterion* in Classical Athens," *Greek, Roman, and Byzantine Studies* 50 [2010]: 507). Also, Korner, "*Ekklēsia* as a Jewish Synagogue Term," 131.

11. The Hebrew word *qahal* in the Old Testament is not always translated as *ekklēsia* in the Greek Old Testament (the Septuagint, or LXX), but *ekklēsia* always translates *qahal*. *Qahal* is a technical term that refers to an actual assembly or gathering of some kind. *TDNT* therefore restricts the definition of *ekklēsia* in the LXX to an actual gathering. "It means 'assembly,' whether in the sense of assembling or of those assembled" (2:527). See also F. L. Hossfeld and E. M. Kindl, "קָהָל: Basic Technical Meaning, The Religious-Cultic Assembly in Dtn/Dtr Texts, *qāhāl* and *'ēdâ* in P, Prophets, Chroniclers History, Psalms, Wisdom," in *Theological Dictionary of the Old Testament*, ed. G. Johannes Botterweck, Helmber Ringgren, and Heinz-Josef Fabry, trans. Douglas Stott (Grand Rapids, MI: Eerdmans, 2003), 12:547, 549, 551; J. Y. Campbell, "The Origin and Meaning of the Christian Use of the Word EKKLHSIA," *Journal of Theological Studies* 49 (1948): 133.

12. See Paul R. House, *Old Testament Theology* (Downers Grove, IL: IVP, 1998), 188.

13. Grant Gaines provides a crucial discussion of the term's use in the Old Testament in "One Church in One Location: Questioning the Biblical, Theological, and Historical Claims of the Multi-site Church Movement" (PhD diss., The Southern Baptist Theological Seminary, 2012), 47–66.

14. Hence, Edmund Clowney observes, "The 'assembly in the desert' (Acts 7:38) was the definitive assembly for Israel, the covenant-making assembly when God claimed his redeemed people as his own" ("The Biblical Theology of the Church," in *The Church in the Bible and the World: An International Study*, ed. D. A. Carson (Eugene, OR: Wipf and Stock, 2002), 17.

15. E.g., *New International Dictionary of New Testament Theology and Exegesis*, 2nd ed., ed. Moisés Silva, 5 vols. (Grand Rapids, MI: Zondervan, 2014), 2:136.

16. *Ekklēsia* in the Greek New Testament translates only the Hebrew word *qahal*, and "there is no good evidence that in the Old Testament *qahal* ever means anything but an actual assembly or meeting of some kind" (J. Y. Campbell, "The Origin and Meaning of the Christian Use of the Word EKKLHSIA," *Journal of Theological Studies* 49 [1948]: 133). See also Gaines's helpful discussion in "One Church in One Location," 48–53.

17. Scholars debate whether the Greco-Roman or Septuagintal background is primary in the New Testament's usage of *ekklēsia*. I believe good hermeneutics requires us to treat the Septuagint as primary (let Scripture interpret Scripture). That said, it also seems naive to disregard common usage. I appreciate G. K. Beale's conclusion that "the early Christian 'assembly' (usually translated church) is the continuation of the true Israelite 'assembly of God' in the new covenant age, which *implicitly* stands in contrast, or as an alternative, to the civic 'assemblies of the world'" ("The Background of ἐκκλησία Revisited," *Journal for the Study of the New Testament* 38, no. 2 [2015]: 166).

18. J. Nolland, *The Gospel of Matthew: A Commentary on the Greek Text* (Grand Rapids, MI: Eerdmans, 2005), 673.

19. Gaines, "One Church in One Location," 64.

20. K. L. Schmidt argues that the decision to use "*ekklēsia*" by the early Christians depended more on the "sacred" influence of the LXX than on the "secular" usage of classical Greek. He argues that the "the ἐκκλησία of the ancient δῆμος is a formal parallel from the secular world, but it corresponds only in the sense of an analogy, no more and no less, just as κύριος Καῖσαρ [Caesar is Lord] is a (polemical) parallel to κύριος Χριστός [Christ is Lord] not its prototype" (*TDNT*, 2:514). But it's not clear to me why we would not see the influence from both domains on the decision to use this word. For starters, citizens of the first century (whether Greek or Jew) would not have seen the same clean division between secular and sacred, just as they would not have seen such a clean division between religious or

cultic and political, as mentioned above. Yes, the claim that "Jesus is Lord" was built on Old Testament categories, but it also very much meant to contradict all other false claimants to the title, including Caesar. So with the *ekklēsia* of God in Christ. It may have been difficult for first-century Hellenistic Jews to have heard the word without hearing *both* classical Greek and scriptural resonances.

21. The word "anything" in context refers to judicial matters (Craig Blomberg, *Matthew*, New American Commentary [Nashville: Broadman & Holman, 1992], 281).

22. J. D. Greear, "A Pastor Defends His Multisite Church," 9Marks, February 25, 2010, https://www.9marks.org/article/pastor-defends-his-multi-site -church/.

23. Thanks to Matthew Sleeman for this point.

24. I believe we can say that Jesus's presence seals everything that occurs in this episode up to this point as we trace the argument through the connecting phrases in Matt. 18:15–20. Vv. 15–17 provide instruction. "Truly, I said to you" says that v. 18 will *ground* the final action taken in v. 17. "Again I say to you" says that v. 19 will *explain* everything in vv. 15–18. "For" says that v. 20 *grounds* v. 19 and, by extension, vv. 15–18 since v. 19 explains them.

25. See Patrick Schreiner's helpful discussion of the meaning of Christ's presence in *The Body of Jesus: A Spatial Analysis of Kingdom in Matthew*, Library of New Testament Studies (New York: Bloomsbury T&T Clark, 2016), 147–50.

26. Both words have as much spatial resonance in the Greek as they do in English.

27. Thanks to Bobby Jamieson for this language. See Jamieson, *Going Public: Why Baptism Is Required for Church Membership* (Nashville: B&H, 2015).

28. It's true that I am a congregationalist, but I borrow the emergency scenario from Presbyterian James Bannerman, who observes that the church whose pastors all die "must have within themselves all power competent to carry on the necessary functions and offices of a Church." Bannerman, *The Church of Christ* (1869; Carlisle, PA: Banner of Truth, 2015), 273.

29. See Thomas White and John Mark Yeats, *Franchising McChurch: Feeding Our Obsession with Easy Christianity* (Colorado Springs: Cook, 2009), 175.

30. *TDNT*, 2:506, 535.

Chapter 2: A Church Is an Assembly

1. I did not include citations of "church" in the plural, e.g., "churches of Galatia" (Gal. 1:2).

2. *Theological Dictionary of the New Testament*, ed. Gerhard Kittel and Gerhard Friedrich, trans. Geoffrey W. Bromiley, 10 vols. [Grand Rapids, MI: Eerdmans, 1964–1976], 2:505, hereafter, *TDNT*.

3. Walter Bauer, *A Greek-English Lexicon of the New Testament and Other Early Christian Literature*, trans. and adapted William F. Arndt and

F. Wilbur Gingrich, ed. F. Wilbur Gingrich and Frederick W. Danker (Chicago: University of Chicago Press, 1979).

4. Walter Bauer, *A Greek-English Lexicon of the New Testament and Other Early Christian Literature*, trans. and adapted William F. Arndt and F. Wilbur Gingrich (Chicago: University of Chicago Press, 1957), 240.

5. In chronological order, Greville Ewing, *A Greek and English Lexicon, Originally a Scripture Lexicon, and Now Adapted to the Greek Classics*, 3rd ed. (Glasgow: University Press, 1827), 375–76; Edward Robinson, *Greek and English Lexicon of the New Testament* (Boston: Crocker and Brewster, 1836), 250; George Ricker Berry, *A New Greek-English Lexicon to the New Testament* (New York: Hinds, Noble & Eldridge, 1897), 69–70; Joseph Henry Thayer, *A Greek-English Lexicon of the New Testament*, corrected ed. (New York: American Book, 1886), 195–96; W. J. Hickie, *Greek-English Lexicon to the New Testament* (New York: Macmillan, 1908), 57; E. W. Bullinger, *A Critical Lexicon and Concordance to the English and Greek New Testament* (1908; repr., Grand Rapids, MI: 1999), 153.

6. *A Greek-English Lexicon to the New Testament*, rev. ed., ed. Thomas Sheldon Green (London: Samuel Bagster & Sons, 1850), 56. This can also be found as the *Analytical Greek Lexicon* (same publisher, 1852), now reprinted as *The New Analytical Greek Lexicon*, ed. Wesley Perschbacher (Peabody, MA: Hendrickson, 1990).

7. John Parkhurst, *A Greek and English Lexicon to the New* Testament, 2nd ed. (London: J. Davis, 1794), 208; S. T. Bloomfield, *A Greek and English Lexicon to the New Testament* (London: Longman, Orme, Brown, Green, & Longmans, 1840), 112–13, which uses the exact same phrasing on this point as does Parkhurst and must have been relying on it; and perhaps G. Abbott-Smith, *A Manual Greek Lexicon of the New Testament* (New York: Charles Scribner's Sons, 1922), 138–39, though it's slightly less clear.

8. According to a biography of John Parkhurst in the fifth edition (1809), the first edition was published in 1769. I could not find it. Parkhurst died in 1797.

9. As evidence, Parkhurst refers to Acts 8:1; 11:22; 1 Cor. 1:2; Col. 4:16; Rev. 1:4, 11, 20; 2:1, 8. He also notes, "From these latter passages of the Revelation it is evident that the number of churches is estimated by the number of *angels* or *bishops*, and that each of these churches was therefore reckoned as one, because governed by one ruler, how many soever were the particular congregations it contained." Parkhurst, *A Greek and English Lexicon*, 208.

10. *TDNT*, 2:534.

11. *TDNT*, 2:503.

12. Geoff Surratt, Greg Ligon, and Warren Bird, *The Multi-site Revolution: Being One Church . . . in Many Locations* (Grand Rapids, MI: Zondervan, 2006), 18.

13. E.g., Gerd Theissen, *The Social Setting of Pauline Christianity: Essays on Corinth* (Philadelphia: Fortress, 1982), 89; Wayne A. Meeks, *The First*

Urban Christians: The Social World of the Apostle Paul (New Haven, CT: Yale University Press, 1983), 75–76; Peter T. O'Brien, *Colossians, Philemon*, Word Biblical Commentary (Waco, TX: Word, 1982), 256–57.

14. Johannes P. Louw and Eugene A. Nida, *Greek-English Lexicon of the New Testament: Based on Semantic Domains*, 2nd ed., vol. 1 (New York: United Bible Societies, 1996), 125, electronic ed.

15. Emanuel Rodriguez, *God's Bible in Spanish: How God Preserved His Words in Spanish through the RVG* (Ontario, CA: Chick, 2010), 55–57.

16. Mark Dever and I lay out a number of reasons why this is the case in *Baptist Foundations: Church Government for an Anti-Institutional Age* (Nashville: B&H Academic, 2015), xv–xvi.

17. Brad House and Gregg Allison, *Multichurch: Exploring the Future of Multisite* (Grand Rapids, MI: Zondervan, 2017), 51–53.

18. See, e.g., Jerome Murphy-O'Connor, *St. Paul's Corinth: Text and Archeology*, 3rd ed. (Collegeville, MN: Liturgical, 2002), 178–85; see floorplans and reconstructions in Roger W. Gehring, *House Church and Mission: The Importance of Household Structures in Early Christianity* (Peabody, MA: Hendrickson, 2004), 313–20.

19. Richard B. Hays, *First Corinthians*, Interpretation: A Bible Commentary for Preaching and Teaching (Louisville: Westminster John Knox, 2011), 6–7.

20. George Eldon Ladd, *A Theology of the New Testament*, rev. ed. (Grand Rapids: Eerdmans, 1993), 577.

21. See Carolyn Osiek and David L. Balch, *Families in the New Testament World: Households and House Churches* (Louisville: Westminster John Knox, 1997), 203. Also Grant Gaines, "One Church in One Location: Questioning the Biblical, Theological, and Historical Claims of the Multi-site Church Movement" (PhD diss., The Southern Baptist Theological Seminary, 2012), 110–15.

22. Edward Adams argues that the early Christians could have met in shops, workshops, barns, warehouses, hotels and inns, and more (*The Earliest Christian Meeting Places: Almost Exclusively Houses?*, rev. ed. [New York: Bloomsbury T&T Clarke, 2016], 137–97).

23. Gehring, *House Church and Mission*, 157. Gehring is not explicitly arguing for the multisite model. He is arguing for a house-church model. But advocates of multisite churches employ the same textual argument, namely, that the New Testament text reveals *both* citywide churches *and* smaller house-church gatherings, which are effectively sites or campuses.

24. Josephus, the first-century Jewish historian, used *ekklēsia* similarly. He used the term to refer not so much to the people as to the people assembled; e.g., "This man got together an assembly [*ekklēsia*]" (F. Josephus, *The Works of Josephus: Complete and Unabridged*, trans. W. Whiston [Peabody, MA: Hendrickson, 1987], 522).

25. Gaines, "One Church in One Location," 52.

26. Gehring, *House Church and Mission*, 134–42; Meeks, *First Urban Christians*, 76; House and Allison, *Multichurch*, 39. See the fascinating reconstruction of the circumstances of seventeen different members of the Corinthian church in Theissen, *Social Setting*, 73–96.

27. Gehring, *House Church and Mission*, 142.

28. Scholar after scholar makes much hay out of the adjective "whole": Gehring, *House Church and Mission*, 157–58; Robert J. Banks, *Paul's Idea of Community*, rev. ed. (Peabody, MA: Hendrickson, 1994), 34; O'Brien, *Colossians, Philemon*, 257; Theissen, *Social Setting*, 89; Meeks, *First Urban Christians*, 75; House and Allison, *Multichurch*, 45–46.

29. Gehring, *House Church and Mission*, 157, emphasis mine.

30. Gehring, *House Church and Mission*, 146.

31. House and Allison make the same assumption: "The church in Rome met in various locations" (*Multichurch*, 39).

32. Gehring, *House Church and Mission*, 144–51. In addition to the three examples listed here, he also points to the families of Aristobulus and Narcissus as two possible house fellowships that belong to other house churches (Rom. 16:10–11).

33. Gehring, *House Church and Mission*, 155.

34. Gehring, *House Church and Mission*, 155.

35. Realize also that people have different convictions about the number of elders in a church. Gehring, for instance, believes that, in Scripture, the household is the primary social institution and metaphor that gives structure to the church. Other biblical metaphors for the church, as well as the citizenship dynamics of Christ's kingdom, take a backseat. That means he believes there is one pastor in every church, just as there is one head to every household. Therefore, where Paul begins Philippians by greeting the "overseers," Gehring assumes that to affirm the city-church, multicongregational model (*House Church and Mission*, 25). Others of us aren't so convinced the household is the primary metaphor for structuring a church, or that churches can have only one pastor.

36. House and Allison, *Multichurch*, 37.

37. House and Allison, *Multichurch*, 39.

38. House and Allison, *Multichurch*, 237n5.

39. Gehring, *House Church and Mission*, 82–83.

40. Clearly Acts 27:35 refers to an ordinary meal. Probably Luke 24:35 does as well, since it was not the disciples' self-conscious participation in the body and blood of Christ.

41. Probably the case in Acts 20:7, 11.

Chapter 3: A Church Should Be Catholic

1. See Andy Johnson, "Pray for Revival—In the Other Guy's Church," 9Marks, May 8, 2012, https://www.9marks.org/article/journalpray-revival-other-guys-church/.

2. See Bobby Jamieson, "The Great Commission Is Bigger Than Your Church," 9Marks, May 8, 2012, https://www.9marks.org/article/journal great-commission-bigger-your-church/.

3. See the excellent work by Thomas White and John Mark Yeats, *Franchising McChurch: Feeding Our Obsession with Easy Christianity* (Colorado Springs: Cook, 2009).

4. Simeon Williams, "Divide and Prosper: A Historical Account of Church-Planting by 'Peaceable Division,'" 9Marks, August 25, 2016, https://www .9marks.org/article/divide-and-prosper-a-historical-account-of-church -planting-by-peaceable-division/.

5. Matthew Spandler-Davison, "Church Planting in the Same Building," 9Marks, June 20, 2017, https://www.9marks.org/article/church-planting -in-the-same-building/. See also Spandler-Davison, "Transitioning Bardstown Christian Fellowship, Bardstown, Kentucky into a Church Planting Network" (DMin diss., The Southern Baptist Theological Seminary, 2015).

6. Colin Clark, "Lessons Learned from Church-Planting by Peaceable Division," 9Marks, June 20, 2017, https://www.9marks.org/article/lessons -learned-from-church-planting-by-peaceable-division/.

7. Mark Dever, "Wanted: Apostolic Pastors," 9Marks, May 8, 2012, https:// www.9marks.org/article/journalwanted-apostolic-pastors-0/.

Appendix 2: Does Acts 9:31 Refer to a Regional "Church"?

1. Anne Rabe holds a PhD in classics from Brown University (2015) and has taught Greek and Latin at a number of institutions, serving most recently as a lecturer at the University of Kansas. She lives in Overland Park, Kansas, with her husband and two children and is a member of Wornall Road Baptist Church, Kansas City, Missouri.

2. The consternation and confusion generated by Luke's use of the singular ἐκκλησία in Acts 9:31 may best be expressed by B. H. Carroll, who states quite bluntly, "To my mind, this is the only use of *ecclesia* in all Biblical or classic literature that is difficult of explanation. The difficulty is frankly expressed" (*Ecclesia—The Church* [Little Rock, AR: Challenge, n.d.], 36).

3. English Standard Version; all other Scripture translations are my own.

4. Kenneth Gangel, for instance, in his commentary on Acts, remarks, "Here we find one of the few times where Luke uses the word *church* in the universal sense" (*Holman New Testament Commentary: Acts* [Nashville: Broadman and Holman, 1998], 144); cf. a similar note for Acts 9:31 found in the Zondervan *NASB Study Bible*: "*church*. The whole Christian body, including Christians in the districts of Judea, Galilee and Samaria. The singular thus does not here refer to the various congregations but to the church as a whole" (1590). As an example of Acts 9:31 enlisted in support of a multisite ecclesiology, Gregg Allison, *Sojourners and Strangers: The Doctrine of the Church* (Wheaton, IL: Crossway, 2012), sees in this verse evidence of "a 'church' structure above the local church level" (268) and

uses it, furthermore, to remove any obstacles to a multisite model, asserting that the appearance of ἐκκλησία in the singular here undermines arguments *against* the multisite model based on the word's meaning of "assembly" (313–14n47). Numerous responses have been offered to Allison's criticism of such lexically based arguments; see, e.g., Grant Gaines's review of *Sojourners and Strangers* on the Gospel Coalition's website, January 9, 2013, https://www.thegospelcoalition.org/reviews/sojourners _and_strangers/.

5. For the singular ἐκκλησία as denoting a community consisting of these three regions, see K. N. Giles, "Luke's Use of the Term ΈΚΚΛΗΣΙΑ' with Special Reference to Acts 20.28 and 9.31," *New Testament Studies* 31 (1985): 135–42, who comments that "Luke here uses the singular ἐκκλησία of a specific community . . . the one congregation, the church of Jerusalem, which has been dispersed because of persecution" (139); cf., similarly, F. J. A. Hort, *The Christian Ecclesia* (London, 1907), 55–56. The conclusions of Giles and Hort are followed by many recent commentators, e.g., David G. Peterson, *The Acts of the Apostles*, The Pillar New Testament Commentary (Grand Rapids, MI: Eerdmans, 2009), 17–18, as well as Darrell L. Bock, *Acts*, Baker Exegetical Commentary on the New Testament (Grand Rapids, MI: Baker Academic, 2007), 372. John B. Polhill, *Acts: An Exegetical and Theological Exposition of Holy Scripture*, The New American Commentary (Nashville: Broadman and Holman, 1992), allows for both interpretations, though he leans toward reading ἐκκλησία as describing a community, namely, "the Jerusalem church pictured in its witness, which extended throughout all these regions" (244). Avoiding the fray nearly completely, F. F. Bruce, *The Book of the Acts*, rev. ed., The New International Commentary on the New Testament (Grand Rapids, MI: Eerdmans, 1988), prefers simply to observe that "Luke uses the singular 'church' here where Paul prefers to use the plural and to speak of 'the churches of Judaea' (Gal. 1:22; cf. 1 Thess. 2:14)" (196).

6. Giles, referring to the noun ἐκκλησία, states that "in the singular [Luke] always uses it of a specific local congregation and when he must speak of congregations in several towns he uses the plural. If the singular is preferred we have a unique use of the word in the New Testament" ("Luke's Use of the Term ΈΚΚΛΗΣΙΑ,'" 138–39).

7. Giles, "Luke's Use of the Term ΈΚΚΛΗΣΙΑ,'" 138.

8. All Greek in this appendix is taken from Nestlé-Aland, *Novum Testamentum Graece*, 28th ed. (Stuttgart: Deutsche Bibelgesellschaft, 2012).

9. γνωστὸν δὲ ἐγένετο *καθ᾽ ὅλης τῆς Ἰόππης* καὶ ἐπίστευσαν πολλοὶ ἐπὶ τὸν κύριον (Acts 9:42).

10. ὑμεῖς οἴδατε τὸ γενόμενον ῥῆμα *καθ᾽ ὅλης τῆς Ἰουδαίας*, ἀρξάμενος ἀπὸ τῆς Γαλιλαίας μετὰ τὸ βάπτισμα ὃ ἐκήρυξεν Ἰωάννης, Ἰησοῦν τὸν ἀπὸ Ναζαρέθ, ὡς ἔχρισεν αὐτὸν ὁ θεὸς πνεύματι ἁγίῳ καὶ δυνάμει (Acts 10:37–38).

11. Καὶ ὑπέστρεψεν ὁ Ἰησοῦς ἐν τῇ δυνάμει τοῦ πνεύματος εἰς τὴν Γαλιλαίαν. καὶ φήμη ἐξῆλθεν *καθ' ὅλης τῆς περιχώρου* περὶ αὐτοῦ (Luke 4:14).

12. οἱ δὲ ἐπίσχυον λέγοντες ὅτι ἀνασείει τὸν λαὸν διδάσκων *καθ' ὅλης τῆς Ἰουδαίας* (Luke 23:5).

13. . . . ἐπὶ ἀρχιερέως Ἄννα καὶ Καιάφα, ἐγένετο *ῥῆμα θεοῦ* ἐπὶ Ἰωάννην τὸν Ζαχαρίου υἱὸν ἐν τῇ ἐρήμῳ (Luke 3:2).

14. On the punctiliar nature of the aorist, see Friedrich Blass, Albert Debrunner, and Robert W. Funk, *A Greek Grammar of the New Testament and Other Early Christian Literature* (Chicago: University of Chicago Press, 1961), § 318, hereafter, BDF. Notice that this is very different from, in fact quite the opposite of, say, an iterative imperfect, which would have indicated here repeated revelations from the Lord to John.

15. If the move from speech acts to churches seems jarring, keep in mind that the church—in its universal form and in local expressions—is itself the product of a divine speech act. God *calls* us to him and to eternal life. Throughout the New Testament the verb καλέω ("call") points not only to a mere invitation extended by God but also to his sovereign role in choosing us and appointing us for salvation—see, e.g., Gal. 5:8 for God as "he who calls"; and for those who follow him as "the called," see 1 Thess. 2:12; 1 Tim. 6:12; and Heb. 9:15. That the Lord's "calling" goes hand in hand with election is made clear in such passages as Rom. 8:30 and 9:11–12 (cf., similarly, Isa. 41:8–9 in the LXX), where καλέω is intertwined with language more explicit of election and predestination (προορίζω, ἐκλογή, ἐκλέγω). And of course καλέω lies at the root of ἐκκλησία—we the church are those who have been "called out" (ἐκ + καλέω) from every tribe, tongue, and nation (Rev. 5:9). Moreover, note that in fact there seems to be a clear distinction between the types of activities that govern κατά in its spatial sense of "throughout" and the similar διά with the genitive as "through" (again, specifically in spatial use): διά is governed nearly exclusively by verbs of motion—compounds of ἔρχομαι, βαίνω, χωρέω, and πορεύομαι (cf., e.g., Matt. 2:12; 12:43; 19:24; Mark 2:23; 10:25; 11:16; Luke 4:30; 5:19; 18:25; John 4:4; 10:1–2; Rom. 15:28; 2 Cor. 11:33 [here the verb χαλάω]; Heb. 11:28)—while κατά is exclusive to speech acts; cf. that in addition to the five verses explored in this appendix (Acts 9:31; 9:42; 10:37; Luke 4:14; 23:5), speech acts govern the prepositional phrases in Luke 8:39 and Acts 13:49 as well, both of which feature phraseology similar to the verses under consideration here (i.e., κατά + acc./διά + gen. as "through," and both modifying the object of the preposition with ὅλος). Many thanks to classics professor Anthony Corbeill for helping me to draw the connection between speech acts and churches.

16. I use the term "iterative" here and throughout knowing that it is otherwise normally applied to verb tenses, not to nouns or prepositions. But I do so both purposefully, to capture the sense of repetition that κατά plus the

genitive here imparts, and also because "distributive"(for lack of a better term), sometimes used in classifying spatial uses of prepositions, seems to me not to be appropriate to the context of speech acts or churches.

17. Compare this to the other instances of the singular ἐκκλησία in Acts often considered to denote the universal church, namely, Acts 5:11 and 20:28. In 5:11, the universalizing sense of ἐκκλησία is made clear through the adjective "whole" (ὅλην) applied to it—καὶ ἐγένετο φόβος μέγας ἐφ᾽ ὅλην τὴν ἐκκλησίαν καὶ ἐπὶ πάντας τοὺς ἀκούοντας ταῦτα (Acts 5:11); and in 20:28, a verse inherently discounted by Giles as failing to reflect Luke's own theology (Giles, "Luke's Use of the Term ΕΚΚΛΗΣΙΑ,'" 140), the tacking on of the qualifying phrase "of God" (or "of the Lord" in some manuscripts) to ἐκκλησία lends a similar sense—τὴν ἐκκλησίαν τοῦ θεοῦ (or τοῦ κυρίου).

18. I hesitate to label this a collective singular decisively, for under the heading of "collective singular" (or *constructio ad sensum*) New Testament grammars document only instances in which (1) a plurality of persons is represented by a singular collective noun, whereby the noun itself is not felt to be plural while reading singular (as in "churches" for the singular ἐκκλησία) but, rather, encompasses in itself a plurality of persons, for instance ὄχλος, πλῆθος, and λαός; cf., e.g., John 6:2 (ἠκολούθει δὲ αὐτῷ ὄχλος πολύς, ὅτι ἐθεώρουν τὰ σημεῖα ἃ ἐποίει ἐπὶ τῶν ἀσθενούντων); cf. also Mark 3:7; Luke 2:13; Acts 21:36; etc. (see BDF, §134); or (2) the singular represents a generic type of person, e.g., Matt. 12:35—ὁ ἀγαθὸς ἄνθρωπος ἐκ τοῦ ἀγαθοῦ θησαυροῦ ἐκβάλλει ἀγαθά, καὶ ὁ πονηρὸς ἄνθρωπος ἐκ τοῦ πονηροῦ θησαυροῦ ἐκβάλλει πονηρά (see BDF, §139). In classical authors the collective singular can designate a plurality of things as well as persons and can truly bear the force of a plural (see Herbert Weir Smyth, *Greek Grammar*, rev. Gordon M. Messing [Cambridge, MA: Harvard University Press, 1956], § 995; cf. Xenophon's *Anabasis* 1.7, where the singular "shield" [ἀσπίς] is clearly used with the force of a plural—Ἐνταῦθα δὴ ἐν τῇ ἐξοπλισίᾳ ἀριθμὸς ἐγένετο τῶν μὲν Ἑλλήνων ἀσπὶς μυρία καὶ τετρακοσία); and were instances of similar usage forthcoming in the New Testament, I would consider offering Acts 9:31 as an additional example. More will be said on this in note 22, to follow. Note that B. H. Carroll briefly entertained the notion that ἐκκλησία in Acts 9:31 represents a collective singular (as put forth apparently by one Meyer), but he presented no philological analysis from the Greek and ultimately dismissed the possibility (Carroll, *Ecclesia*, 38–39).

19. The distinctively Lukan nature of κατά used with the genitive to express "throughout" is noted in New Testament grammars and lexica (e.g., Walter Bauer, Frederick W. Danker, William F. Arndt, and F. Wilbur Gingrich, *A Greek-English Lexicon of the New Testament and Other Early Christian Literature*, 3rd ed. [Chicago: University of Chicago Press, 2000], s.v. κατά; BDF, §225). This phenomenon is in fact so particular to Luke that is it not only confined to books of his authorship in the New Testament but also un-

attested in classical usage. The standard lexicon for classical Greek—Liddell and Scott's *Greek-English Lexicon*—does not even offer "throughout" as a possible meaning for κατά with the genitive, nor does Smyth's *Greek Grammar*. Note too that all four parallel instances, as well as Acts 9:31, also modify the object of κατά (namely, the specific geographical regions) with the adjective ὅλης ("whole" or "all of"), thus creating an even stronger linguistic connection between the five instances and forming a phraseology all the more distinct.

20. I.e., αἱ . . . ἐκκλησίαι . . . εἶχον . . . οἰκοδομούμεναι . . . πορευόμεναι . . . ἐπληθύνετο. The singular ἐκκλησία appears in such editions as Nestle-Aland's *Novum Testamentum Graece*, 28th ed. (Stuttgart: Deutsche Bibelgesellschaft, 2012); Tyndale House's *The Greek New Testament* (Wheaton, IL: Crossway, 2017), and Wescott and Hort's *The Greek New Testament* (Peabody, MA: Hendrickson, 2007); even the Vulgate prints the singular. The plural ἐκκλησίαι can be found, e.g., in *The Greek New Testament according to the Majority Text*, ed. Z. C. Hodges and A. L. Farstad (Nashville: Thomas Nelson, 1982). For a more thorough list of editions that print the plural, see Giles, "Luke's Use of the Term ΕΚΚΛΗΣΙΑ,'" 142n22. A helpfully summarizing note on the matter in general may be found in Peterson, *Acts of the Apostles*, 317–18n78.

21. Cf. Bruce Metzger's note on Acts 9:31 in *A Textual Commentary on the Greek New Testament*, 2nd ed. (Stuttgart: Deutsche Bibelgesellschaft, 1994), 322–23. Metzger advocates reading the singular ἐκκλησία here based on the quality of the manuscripts that bear this reading and the reasoning that, as an original reading, the singular is much more likely to have been changed into a plural for the sake of conformity with other passages than the plural to the singular. Giles too defends the singular ἐκκλησία as the proper reading ("Luke's Use of the Term ΕΚΚΛΗΣΙΑ,'" 138–40).

22. The plural variant ἐκκλησίαι has otherwise been explained as an attempt to align Acts 9:31 with 15:41 and 16:5, where Luke uses the plural form in reference to multiple geographical regions (see, e.g., Metzger, *Textual Commentary*, 323, and Giles, "Luke's Use of the Term ΕΚΚΛΗΣΙΑ,'" 139). Giles's treatment of Acts 9:31 warrants further discussion here, for he provides an extended consideration of the manuscript tradition of this verse and weighs the various options presented by the manuscripts—all singular readings, all plural readings, and a singular noun with plural verbs and participles (138–40). Giles ultimately comes down in favor of the last of these, proposing that Acts 9:31 originally contained the singular ἐκκλησία with *masculine* plural participles and plural verb forms, and he suggests that these masculine plural forms denote the scattered members of the Jerusalem church (139), pointing to the combination of singular ἐκκλησία and plural verbs that occurs in Acts 8:1 (ἐγένετο δὲ ἐν ἐκείνῃ τῇ ἡμέρᾳ διωγμὸς μέγας ἐπὶ τὴν ἐκκλησίαν τὴν ἐν Ἱεροσολύμοις, πάντες δὲ διεσπάρησαν κατὰ

τὰς χώρας τῆς Ἰουδαίας καὶ Σαμαρείας πλὴν τῶν ἀποστόλων). I see two problems with this conclusion, however.

First, the singular-plural combination in Acts 8:1 is not at all similar to what Giles proposes for Acts 9:31. At 8:1, the plural διεσπάρησαν logically follows its subject (πάντες), and these plurals (along with those in the following verses) represent a new and distinct group from the church at Jerusalem: the scattered. This may seem obvious, but it is crucial to see that Luke, from this point on in his narrative, distinguishes between (1) the remaining church in Jerusalem (Luke clearly tells us that at least a few people remained—πάντες . . . πλὴν ἀποστόλων, Acts 8:1) and (2) those who were scattered. The scattered, once members of the church, represented by the plurals, now constitute a separate category; notice that Luke *continues* to speak of the church in Jerusalem (again, as always, in the singular) in its remnant state only two verses later (Acts 8:3). So what we in fact see in the opening four verses of Acts 8 is Luke switching back and forth in his narrative between the remnant church and its scattered former members, focusing on the story of the latter exclusively from v. 4 on. In short, the plurals in 8:1ff. do not refer to the church in Jerusalem.

Second, and most importantly, although the combination of the singular ἐκκλησία and masculine plurals would accord well with the *constructio ad sensum* variety of collective singular—that in which the singular represents a plurality of people that can then be conceived of and represented grammatically as a plurality through (masculine) plural forms (see note 18 above)—the noun ἐκκλησία in particular is otherwise nowhere attested in this usage. Given that ἐκκλησία seems as likely a candidate for such treatment as the nouns that routinely appear in this construction (again, ὄχλος, πλῆθος, and λαός, but also οἰκία and στρατία; see BDF, §134), that ἐκκλησία is *not* used this way (and Giles offers no parallels), although an *argumentum ex silentio*, still argues loudly against Giles's suggestion. Surely if Luke had once used the singular ἐκκλησία collectively, he and other New Testament authors—all of whom employ *constructio ad sensum* regularly— would have done so elsewhere. In fact I suggest that they don't, precisely because of the argument presented throughout this book: ἐκκλησία was felt so strongly to comprise a whole, gathered assembly that New Testament authors by instinct never strayed mentally and grammatically to its multiple, individual members, and therefore to plurals. To do so would have been contrary to the sense of the word itself.

23. Note that this argument is very specific to Luke's distinctive phrasing in the Greek and does not necessarily extend to English phrases like "the church throughout Kansas," though native English speakers may still understand plurals in such instances.

24. Gangel, *Acts*, 144.

GENERAL INDEX

SCRIPTURE INDEX

9Marks

Building Healthy Churches

9Marks exists to equip church leaders with a biblical vision and practical resources for displaying God's glory to the nations through healthy churches.

To that end, we want to see churches characterized by these nine marks of health:

1. Expositional Preaching
2. Biblical Theology
3. A Biblical Understanding of the Gospel
4. A Biblical Understanding of Conversion
5. A Biblical Understanding of Evangelism
6. Biblical Church Membership
7. Biblical Chuch Discipline
8. Biblical Discipleship
9. Biblical Church Leadership

Find all our Crossway titles and other resources at 9Marks.org.

IX 9Marks

crossway.org